Poetry of the First World War

LONGMAN ENGLISH SERIES

This series includes both period anthologies and selections from the work of individual authors. The introductions and notes have been based upon the most up-to-date criticism and scholarship and the editors have been chosen for their special knowledge of the material.

General Editor   Maurice Hussey

Poetry 1900 to 1965 *Edited by George MacBeth*
(Published jointly with Faber and Faber)
Poetry of the First World War *Edited by Maurice Hussey*
Poetry of the 1940s *Edited by Howard Sergeant*
A Selection from George Crabbe *Edited by John Lucas*
The Byronic Byron *Edited by Gilbert Phelps*
Victorian Poetry 1830 to 1870 *Edited by Patrick Scott*
Gulliver's Travels *Edited by Angus Ross*
A Selection from John Keats *Edited by E.C. Pettet*

Poetry of
the First World War

An anthology selected and edited by

Maurice Hussey

Longman

LONGMAN GROUP LIMITED

London

*Associated companies, branches and representatives
throughout the world*

*Introduction and notes © Longman Group Ltd
(formerly Longmans, Green & Co. Ltd) 1967
First published 1967
Reprinted wuth corrections 1971
Seventh impression 1979*

ISBN 0 582 34152 3

*Printed in Hong Kong by
Wing Tai Cheung Printing Co Ltd*

THE EDITOR

Maurice Hussey is Principal Lecturer in English at the
Cambridgeshire College of Arts and Technology and
General Editor of 'Longman English Series' and
'Preface Books'. His publications upon Chaucer have
been widely disseminated and his most recent publi-
cation is the revised edition of *Chester Mystery Plays*
(Heinemann) which was the basis of his script for the
B.B.C. Television production of Easter 1976.

For my mother
with all love

Contents

Acknowledgements

First of all I should record my indebtedness to those with the closest personal connections with my subject: Mr Dyneley Hussey and the brothers of two dead writers, Mr Ronald Gurney and Mr Kenneth Sorley. To Mr Gurney goes my special gratitude for sanctioning the study and use of the unpublished MSS of Ivor Gurney.

Two most knowledgeable friends who have offered me several useful suggestions, Mr Sydney Bolt, editor of the companion anthology *The Poetry of the 1920s* in which the post-war work of a number of the poets included here can be traced, and Professor D. S. R. Welland, author of the well-known study of Wilfred Owen's output.

The critics who have been of most assistance to myself, and will greatly help all my readers, have included J. K. Johnston, whose *English Poetry in the First World War* is the first modern full-length account of its topic; and Bernard Bergonzi, whose still more perceptive *Heroes' Twilight* (1965) has the additional advantage of studying also the prose writings. To these I should add Mr Edgell Rickword whose criticism of the poetry of the period has been as valuable as his personal contribution to it.

To my friend Surendra Agarwala goes continuous gratitude for a great deal of typing spread over a considerable period.

For permission to reprint the poetry in their copyright the Editor and Publishers are indebted to the following persons and companies:

George Allen & Unwin Ltd for 'In the Trenches' and 'Soliloquy I and II' from *Collected Poems* by Richard Aldington, and 'God, How I Hate You' and 'Night Patrol' from *The Diary of a Dead Officer* by Arthur Graeme West; Mrs George Bambridge and Methuen & Co. Ltd for 'For all we have and are' and '*Epitaphs of the War*': 'Bombed in London', 'A Dead Statesman', 'The Favour', 'A Son' and 'Unknown Female Corpse' from *The Years Between* by Rudyard Kipling; The Bodley Head Ltd for 'Germania' by Eden Phillpotts from *Wild Fruit, Poems, etc.* and 'Recruiting' by E. A. Mackintosh from *War the Liberator* (1918); Cambridge University Press for 'All the hills and vales along', 'To Germany' and 'When you see millions of the mouthless dead' from *Marlborough and Other Poems* by Charles Hamilton

Sorley; Jonathan Cape Ltd for 'Armageddon—and After' by Laurence Housman; Chatto & Windus Ltd for 'Anthem for Doomed Youth', 'At a Calvary near the Ancre', 'From my Diary, July 1914', 'Futility', 'The Next War', 'The Parable of the Old Man and the Young', 'The Send-Off' and 'Strange Meeting' by Wilfred Owen, and 'Break of Day in the Trenches', 'Dead Man's Dump', 'Louse Hunting' and 'Marching' by Isaac Rosenberg; Mr Alan Denson, Literary Executor of the late Herbert E. Palmer for 'Air Raids: 1917–1918' by Herbert Edward Palmer; Gerald Duckworth & Co. Ltd for 'Carrion' from *Collected Poems* by Harold Monro, and 'Judas and the Profiteer' and 'The Modern Abraham' from *Collected Satires and Poems of Osbert Sitwell*; the author for 'Five Souls' by W. N. Ewer; Faber & Faber Ltd for 'A Note on War Poetry' from *Collected Poems 1909–1962* by T. S. Eliot, 'Dooleysprudence' from *Critical Writings of James Joyce* edited by E. Mason and R. Ellman, 'Hugh Selwyn Mauberley Part IV' from *Personae* by Ezra Pound, and 'The Happy Warrior', 'Kneeshaw Goes to War IV', 'My Company' and 'Ypres' from *Collected Poems* by Herbert Read; the author and The Bodley Head Ltd for 'What the Orderly Dog Saw' from *Collected Poems* by Ford Madox Ford; Miss Pamela and Miss Ursula Frankau for 'Ammunition Column' from *The Guns*, and 'Poison' from *Poems of War and Peace* by Gilbert Frankau; Miss J. Freeman for 'Happy is England Now' by John Freeman; Mr Michael Gibson and Macmillan & Co. Ltd for 'In the Ambulance', 'The Bayonet' and 'Mad' from *Collected Poems, 1905–1925* by Wilfrid Gibson; Lord Glenconner for 'Home Thoughts from Laventie' by E. W. Tennant; Mr Ronald Gurney for 'Picture of two Veterans', 'When I am Covered' and 'Ypres' from the *Gurney Collection* in the Gloucester Public Library, and 'Dirge for two Striplings', 'Servitude', 'The Target', 'To the Poet before Battle' and 'West Country' by Ivor Gurney; the Trustees of the Hardy Estate and Macmillan & Co. Ltd for 'And there was a great Calm', 'Before Marching and After' and 'Channel Firing' from *The Collected Poems of Thomas Hardy*; Mr Patrick W. H. Harvey for 'Autumn in Prison' and 'If We Return' by F. W. Harvey; Hodder & Stoughton Ltd for 'Nox Mortis' by Paul Bewsher; Holt, Rinehart and Winston Inc. and Jonathan Cape Ltd for 'To E.T.' from *The Complete Poems of Robert Frost*, Copyright 1923, 1928 by Holt, Rinehart and Winston, Inc. Copyright 1951, 1956 by Robert Frost; the author's agents for 'The Call' by R. C. Vernede; the author for 'An Oxford Retrospect: May 1915' by Dyneley Hussey; Hutchinson & Co. (Publishers) Ltd for 'War Books' by Ivor Gurney; International

Authors N.V. for 'Country at War' and 'The Leveller' from *Country Sentiment* by Robert Graves; Mr Joseph Ledwidge for 'After Court Martial' by Francis Ledwidge; Methuen & Co. Ltd for 'Advance on the Somme' and 'Battle of the Marne' by Herbert Trench; Mrs D. M. Mewton-Wood for 'Aeroplanes' by W. J. Turner; Sir Francis Meynell for 'Lord, I owe Thee a Death' by Alice Meynell; John Murray (Publishers) Ltd for 'Before Action' and 'Back to Rest' from *Verse and Prose in Peace and War* by W. N. Hodgson, and 'The Face' and 'A Shell' from *Eidola* by Frederick Manning; Captain Francis Newbolt, C.M.G. for 'Vitai Lampada' by Sir Henry Newbolt from *Poems New and Old* published by John Murray (Publishers) Ltd; A. D. Peters & Co. for 'Zero', 'The Veteran', 'Report on Experience' and 'War Biography—Written in Illness' by Edmund Blunden; Laurence Pollinger Ltd, the Estate of the late Mrs Frieda Lawrence and William Heinemann Ltd for 'We Have Gone Too Far' and 'New Heaven and New Earth—Section IV' from *The Complete Poems of D. H. Lawrence*; G. P. Putnam's Sons for 'From the Somme' by Leslie Coulson from *Valiant Muse* (1936); the author for 'Winter Warfare', 'Trench Poets', 'War and Peace' and 'The Soldier Addresses His Body' from *Collected Poems* (1947) by Edgell Rickword, published by The Bodley Head Ltd; Lady Salmond for 'Into Battle' by Julian Grenfell; the author for 'Aftermath', 'Counter-Attack', 'Does it Matter', 'The Dug-Out', 'The General', 'Lamentations', 'The Rear-Guard' and 'Stretcher Case' by Siegfried Sassoon; the Author's Representatives and Sidgwick & Jackson Ltd for 'On the Wings of the Morning' by Jeffrey Day and 'Three Hills' from *Three Hills and Other Poems* by Everard Owen; The Society of Authors as the literary representative of the Estate of the late Laurence Binyon for 'For the Fallen' by Laurence Binyon; the Society of Authors as the literary representative of the Estate of the late Sir William Watson for 'Sons of Britain' by William Watson; Mrs Helen Thomas for 'Lights Out', 'A Private', 'No One Cares Less than I', 'October' and 'The Trumpet' from *Collected Poems* by Edward Thomas published by Faber and Faber Ltd; and Mr Milton Waldman, Literary Executor of the late Robert Nichols for 'Boy' by Robert Nichols.

We regret that we have been unable to trace the copyright owner in 'When it's Over' by Max Plowman and would welcome any information that would enable us to do so.

Authors and poems

Preface

The poetry represented in this book, the work of many hands, may for a moment be approached as that of one composite writer, the English war poet. This man's mind can be seen developing as the conduct of the war makes certain ideas less and less tenable. The first mood, a patriotic prompting, drove the young writer from school or college to join the colours; it attains, poetic form in the stilted rhetoric and the radiant assurance of untested ideals. In the second place, he begins to find reasons for becoming tentative in his patriotism and withdrawing into a more meditative position; he learns to look into his heart and write with a greater honesty. At another point, either after the Battle of the Somme in 1916 or in 1917—with the appointment of Field Marshal Haig to the supreme position in the British Army—the bloodshed and misery intensify: the outcome seems no more certain nor more swiftly attainable. Protest against the continuance of hostilities makes the old romanticism both blind and morally objectionable. There emerges from all the experience a moment in which the writer ceases to be the moralist and accepts the state of war as the inevitable condition against which the individual's struggle is fruitless.

These moods are to be found dispersed throughout the anthology, which collects together what one writer called the elegies of a whole generation.

The book is planned in three parts, 'Before Marching,' 'Marching' and 'After Marching,' each with a brief introduction, followed by an 'Afterword' and biographical notes on the poets represented. The alphabetical arrangement may prevent readers from making too swift an equation of poets' opinions and attitudes, and the resultant scatter of the poems encourages a more gradual assimilation of the theme from a mass of conflicting tendencies all discernible at the same period when the development of the English lyric was especially rapid.

War Itself

Blue	Smoke	War
White	Bones	Men

TU FU (8th Cent.)

Before Marching

TO THE POET BEFORE MARCHING

Now, youth, the hour of thy dread passion comes;
Thy lovely things must all be laid away;
And thou, as others, must face the riven day
Unstirred by rattle of the rolling drums
Or bugles' strident cry. When mere noise numbs
The sense of being, the sick soul doth sway,
Remember thy great craft's honour, that they may say
Nothing in shame of poets. Then the crumbs
Of praise the little versemen joyed to take
Shall be forgotten; then they must know we are,
For all our skill in words, equal in might
And strong of mettle as those we honoured. Make
The name of poet terrible in just war,
And like a crown of honour upon the fight.

IVOR GURNEY

And After

I knew a man, he was my chum
but he grew blacker every day.

EDGELL RICKWORD

1 Before Marching

Fifty years on from World War I, the events still refuse to bury themselves in oblivion. On the contrary, details come closer to us as a result of the investigations of historians, the tactics of journalists and the productions of the television studios. A vast corpus of information and impressions remains available as for no earlier war in European history. It also happens that young readers, for whom anything before 1950 might be classified as ancient history, have grown up with an eye on this period of the past and have become increasingly responsive to its poetry. Where Keats or Shelley might have been the object of devotion in an earlier time, Wilfred Owen has been found to haunt many a young reader unlike anybody else in adult writing.

Developments in the arts and changes in technology have one thing in common: they are easily stirred up by war. The sudden strong experiences of a world at war lead a scientist to his laboratory and a writer to his desk fired with a similar imagination. So it is that the fire and mud of the Western Front in the War inspired a prodigious number of poets. So many, in fact, that one grows slightly amused by one's speculations: could there be a dug-out, a shell-hole or a shelter anywhere in which there was nobody writing at the very least a letter home and at most polishing the third draft of a new poem?

Not all the English poetry of the war was of a high level, nor was the process confined to writing in one language. Men from Canada, Australia and New Zealand were never able to write anything above the level of jingoism and for some reason the work of naval poets was inferior to that of their army colleagues. In France there was the work of Paul Claudel, Guillaume Apollinaire and Charles Péguy, known for his attitude of sanctity towards fighting (*'heureux ceux qui sont morts dans une juste guerre'*).* In Italy there was D'Annunzio, a prophet of violence, and in Russia, Alexander Blok and Mayakovsky before the Russian Revolution of 1917 monopolised their attention.

* 'happy are they who die in a just war'.

Germany, with such poets as Heym, George and Trakl, was a country in which some of the exaggerations and poses of the Expressionist school were closely involved with attitudes towards the war and quite different from the outlooks of writers in English. It would indeed look as though the war poets were all intending, together with Isaac Rosenberg, 'not to leave a corner of [their] consciousness covered up, but to saturate [themselves] with the strange and extraordinary new conditions of [their] life'.

None of the other poets was so uniquely involved as Rosenberg or maintained so stoical an attitude. He was content to explore a world of symbolism in which William Blake might have been at home, avoiding emotional participation in (and almost without reference to) a world at war, making allowance for the basic strangeness of the experiences. It could hardly be a period for wide aesthetic experiment. Poets preferred to use it as a time to state facts, to colour them with the imagination and seek to provoke the pity of the reader. Sometimes the result was more document than literature, but at others it is the excellence of the poetry that is itself the document and the wonder: that a man writing in his dug-out or his shell-hole with explosions all round him could produce this. One thinks of the uncanny detachment of Mozart in the process of creation. Something of this sort happened in the minds of a number of English poets.

The Playing Fields of Clifton

The majority of our writers who form this collection were officers and old public-schoolboys. There were, naturally, exceptions such as Ivor Gurney and, again, Isaac Rosenberg. Julian Grenfell and Osbert Sitwell were both professional soldiers before 1914, though most of the others volunteered and achieved positions of responsibility at an unusually early age. They showed, as a group, intense cheerfulness and bravado, which had no time to abate, and a disregard for self-preservation which added stature to their brief experience. It gave them too a sense of living dangerously that resulted in the great variety of their literary impressions.

Critics now deride public schools, but it is impossible not to notice the self-command and discipline that their young men showed. It was as if their whole education had been purchased just for this and geared especially to it. In a way, one must suppose that it had. On Speech Day the school had always encouraged the ready-made patriotic platitude about the mission of the Empire which most of the boys accepted. This ethos, with its traditions of conservatism, its tinges of cruelty and its zest for passionate male friendship, its idolization of games, flourished on the battlefield and went on permanent record in the poetry. There can be no doubt that the toughness and bullying experienced at many schools hardened the pupils and made them more resilient under war stress than men who had been less privileged and known nothing like it. It has been explained to me, though with irony, that if anybody had gone to Christ's Hospital he would have found many of the discomforts of the trenches as things of naught!

In no other country, one suspects, could a man like Sir Henry Newbolt continue to mistake public school propaganda for adult poems; such is the English infantilism that foreign observers often deride. The notorious 'Vitai Lampada' (p. 15) could nowhere else appear as a serious poem. Another Clifton College boy faces death in a Newbolt poem thus:

> He saw the School Close, sunny and green,
> The runner beside him, the stand by the parapet wall,
> The distant tape, and the crowd roaring between.
>
> *He Fell among Thieves*

Accepting this since we must, with our knowledge of Old Boys' Dinners and Cricket Matches, we can also understand how the colonial wars of the nineteenth century had been won. The Boer War, even, was still seen largely as a game in which the Away team must always be better supplied.

When we reach the personal level, it is undeniably poignant to find young officers imagining that the new war would also be rather fun. It will be remembered that there had been no major war for a century and there was nothing to tell in advance that this would develop into the greatest major war on record. Experts such as bankers and actuaries were sure that victory could be secured in a few months; they were also the men who were taken by surprise when the war broke out in the first place. So, then, we look over the shoulder of a young man named Paul Jones as he writes a letter home. 'I have longed for the rough and tumble of war', he adds, 'as for a football match.' One who survived to look back on the effects of his education and his war service was that indispensable guide to the period, Robert Graves. He knew that it was difficult for young officers who one week had been at school where boys were lonely, philistine and unaware, and the next, leading men into battle. It was as he said in his poem, a 'queer time' and 'The trouble is, things happen much too quick'.

T. S. Eliot, who remained American in outlook, like his friend Ezra Pound, was quite outside this circle and criticised the limitations of the public school mind and its poetry thus: 'The popularity of certain war poems was due, I think, to the fact that they appeared to represent a revolt against something that was very unpleasant and really paid a tribute to the nicest feelings of the upper middle-class British public schoolboy.' But in the end, twenty per cent of all eligible men from these schools were killed in the fighting, having shown themselves both brave and sensitive officers.

The Georgians

There is a further point of departure for the study of the poetry of World War I, one stage through which a great number of poets passed. In literature, though not in architecture, the *Georgian* period refers to the reign of George V which began in 1910. To be more specific, the Georgian years were from 1911 to 1922 when a series of anthologies entitled *Georgian Poetry* were published by Edward Marsh, then secretary to Winston Churchill, First Lord of the Admiralty. This was the stage of apprenticeship that many poets served and the form of publication in which a large readership discovered them. This movement has fallen into discredit today and it is one of the weaknesses of many popular modern anthologies that the Georgian poets should be so widely represented. The most familiar members of this group are W. H. Davies, John Freeman and Rupert Brooke, all minor talents. D. H. Lawrence contributed to the Marsh anthologies before he left England,

4

but Thomas Hardy and Edward Thomas whose subject was suitably rustic were never included.

Georgian Poetry was devoted to the sights and emotions of the countryside and the lyrical, nostalgic word patterns that can be formed from it. One piece of egregious incompetence by John Freeman is typical—we meet him again on p. 63—

> It was the lovely moon that lover-like
> Hovered over the wandering, tired
> Earth, her bosom grey and dove-like,
> Hovering beautiful as a dove.

With one's mind entirely closed to the sense of the poem it would be possible to admire the music or the imagery that invests so heavily in the emotional associations of the moon and the peaceful composure of the dove. The piece ends with a slight rearrangement:

> Of the round, lovely thoughtful moon.

Brooke, whose prewar poems represent his talents at their best, was known to invoke the hills and clouds as his images to help him 'forget the lies and truths and pains'. Edward Thomas, on the other hand, wrote nature poetry in which he refused to be shielded, but was still doubtful of the meaning of his own experiences. Yet he writes without nostalgia or bathos:

> How dreary-swift, with naught to travel to
> Is Time. I cannot bite the day to the core.

When we read one of Thomas's nature pieces we are inclined to ask ourselves this: Why is country poetry so frequently naïve? Isn't there room for adult writing on the countryside? Since Thomas was capable of complex thought in such surroundings, why must so much pastoral poetry resemble what the music critic, Constant Lambert, once remarked of the composer Vaughan Williams, 'a cow looking over a gate'? Gloucestershire, the home of both Thomas and Vaughan Williams, was especially well provided with writers before the war. Ivor Gurney and F. W. Harvey, two other poets represented in this volume, were born there, and the distinguished American writer, Robert Frost, lived and published his first poetry from a home in that county. Lascelles Abercrombie, another Georgian living at that time in the same area, was host to many others and created a school known as the Ryton poets from the name of Abercrombie's village.

The mention of Vaughan Williams serves to remind us that music had its Georgian pastorals as well. Edward Elgar, the imperialist, the Kipling of music, lived in the next county, writing a quantity of wartime patriotic music which was a logical development from the peacetime works he had composed already. Vaughan Williams was a contrast. His typical sound is not brassy but rhapsodic, pastoral and impregnated with folksong. Though he studied with the artificial and witty Maurice Ravel, one cannot with certainty pick out a phrase that seems to have been the outcome of any Gallic influence. It was possible before 1914 to know of Schoenberg and his school of composition in Vienna, but Vaughan Williams was not the man to know of it for thirty years, or when he did, to approve. His music is the exact counterpart of Georgian poetry that remained similarly unchanged by the impact of Eliot and Pound and unaffected by the postwar climate of opinion. The only music of protest known to me written during the war is Delius's 'Requiem' which should be revived.

For Vaughan Williams, however, there was a point at which an aggressive note grew up inside his music, the equivalent, perhaps, of his thoughts during war service. This came in 1934 in his Symphony No. 4 in F minor, a work of rare strength which may suggest the sounds of war or the influence of Bartók. But the composer affected not to like or understand his own score, and this protest, twenty years incubating, was stifled, the note of aggressiveness being intermittent thereafter.

The Georgians were too placid. What was designed as a liberation of the arts from the propaganda of imperialism relapsed into complacency. All a true Georgian could do was to repeat himself, and since there was financial reward for such repetitions, there was no reason for him to provide anything else. The Georgian poet Siegfried Sassoon was a long time adjusting his poetic powers to his discovery of trench warfare and when he had found the phrases, he was again at an impasse in 1918, wanting to return to them again in peacetime. Paul Nash, the Georgian painter, who turned from country scenes to the battlefields with great distinction, was similarly stranded after the end of hostilities, describing himself as a 'war artist without a war'. Most Georgians found to their cost that they were becoming inflexible. War poetry and pastoral poetry alike were constrictions upon the poet, ways of excluding too much of human experience. Robert Graves, now seventy, has always been an explorer. He found another way out. He dismissed the output of a whole decade as youthful enthusiasm and removed virtually all his early work, the Georgian and the military together, from his reprinted collections. To him it is an episode that he like most other writers went through. Today, a writer might consider drugs; in the past he opted for the countryside and the old nostalgia.

August 1914

The question of responsibility for the outbreak of war in 1914 is still not settled, in spite of a plethora of historical papers devoted to it. Where it was originally imputed to the German spirit of aggressiveness alone, it is now accepted that while the rise of Germany constituted a threat to other nations on her borders, the two systems of alliances already built up made an outbreak inevitable. As the French sociologist, Raymond Aron, wrote in 1954, 'The two camps alarmed each other and each tried to soothe its own fears by piling up defensive armaments'. Into this tense world in July 1914 drove Archduke Franz Ferdinand to inspect the Bosnian Army at Sarajevo, and incidentally in A. J. P. Taylor's memorable phrase, 'to show off his Archduchess'; in effect to be assassinated.

The ensuing German attack on the borders of Belgium rendered the English entry into the war inevitable. Even so, it is far from certain that the major nations of Europe were ready, although political prophets had foreseen it. For England it came at the end of a sweltering hot summer month when nobody was prepared and everybody was on holiday. There seemed to be enough trouble at home already to occupy those seriously inclined towards politics. Strikes in many major industries were a portent and the Irish revolt in support of Home Rule refused to die down, no matter what else was happening. It was feared in some quarters that international anarchists, egged on by believers in proletarian violence already in the country, were choosing this moment to strike. The Liberal government in power was aware of great areas of discontent which remained under the surface and hoped that they could be swiftly cleared away. To provide still more unwanted diversion, this was the moment the suffragettes chose to demonstrate in support of their demand for votes for women. The clash of international hostilities brought fear to the country but no unity in the national effort.

One might hardly have expected poetry to play any role at such a moment. Much later a government official decided that since poetry was becoming an embarrassment it ought to have been banned. But in August 1914 while there were poets of the type of William Watson there was a purpose for poetry in recruiting propaganda. Virtually every newspaper—possibly for the last time in this country—carried poems, out of which a Christmas volume, *Songs and Sonnets for England in Wartime*, was derived. The poems by Watson (p. 141) and Phillpotts (p. 104) are of this variety with imagery from a much older war and rhetoric based on the great (mainly naval) commanders of the past. It looks now as though these poets were like generals responding to tanks and planes with cavalry and bows and arrows.

The effect of the propaganda was overwhelming. Reception centres had neither the huts to house the men nor the uniforms to clothe them, and a number of them had to drill in their own clothes or simply wait to be taken in. At such a time there was no question of the validity of the war and no criticism of policy except for its hasty improvisation. Nobody at home was allowed to know that deadlock was soon encountered on the battlefront and everyone was confidently assured that 'the boys will all be home for Christmas'.

Prewar Poems

In this section, for historical interest and for contrast, are grouped some poems composed up to the summer of 1914.

The earliest are the most unexpected and need introduction. Walt Whitman is included because he fought in the American Civil War, a conflict that was equally fought between members of the same race. English fighting during the same period was mainly between races with different colours of skin. Whitman was a stretcher-bearer though he proclaimed 'I am the man, I suffered, I was there'. What is notable about 'Reconciliation' especially is the compassion and humanity of it. It seems to antedate Wilfred Owen by fifty years. It is not likely that it was widely read in this country, although interestingly enough, two Georgians, Ivor Gurney and Vaughan Williams certainly read it. Ivor Gurney wrote several poems in imitation of Whitman, and Vaughan Williams set these lines to music about 1938, though he possibly knew them in 1911 when he first set Whitman to music.

The poems of Austin and Henley were written at the close of the nineteenth century and the opening of the twentieth. W. E. Henley's free verse goes further: in his welcome for physical violence here and in his more famous 'Song of the Sword' ('edged to annihilate'), critics have detected the glimmerings of Fascism. One should not take him too seriously since he was a cripple and found such vicarious destruction his perverse form of self-fulfilment.

Of Newbolt's Clifton College imagery enough has already been said. Edward Thomas, Rupert Brooke, Ivor Gurney and Wilfred Owen are represented here in a prewar stage of development for comparison with their later work. The last seems, with his flourishes of aestheticism, the most old-fashioned. Hardy's 'Channel Firing' is famous for its prophetic subject and we return to him in the section 'Two Civilian Poets'.

9

From Why England is Conservative

ALFRED AUSTIN

I

Because of our dear Mother, the fair Past,
On whom twin Hope and Memory safely lean,
And from whose fostering wisdom none shall wean
Their love and faith, while love and faith shall last:
Mother of happy homes and Empire vast,
Of hamlets meek, and many a proud demesne,
Blue spires of cottage smoke 'mong woodlands green,
And comely altars where no stone is cast.
And shall we barter these for gaping Throne,
Dismantled towers, mean plots without a tree,
A herd of hinds too equal to be free,
Greedy of other's, jealous of their own,
And where sweet Order now breathes cadenced tone,
Envy, and hate, and all uncharity?

II

Banish that fear! 'Twere infamy to yield
To folly what to force had been denied,
Or in the Senate quail before the tide
We should have stemmed and routed in the field.
What though no more we brandish sword and shield,
Reason's keen blade is ready at our side,
And manly brains, in wisdom panoplied,
Can foil the shafts that treacherous sophists wield.
The spirit of our fathers is not quelled.
With weapons valid even as those they bore,
Domain, Throne, Altar, still may be upheld,
So we disdain, as they disdained of yore,
The foreign froth that foams against our shore,
Only by its white cliffs to be repelled!

The Hill

RUPERT BROOKE

Breathless, we flung us on the windy hill,
   Laughed in the sun, and kissed the lovely grass.
   You said, 'Through glory and ecstasy we pass;
Wind, sun, and earth remain, the birds sing still,
When we are old, are old . . .' 'And when we die
   All's over that is ours; and life burns on
Through other lovers, other lips,' said I,
   'Heart of my heart, our heaven is now, is won!'

'We are Earth's best, that learnt her lesson here.
   Life is our cry. We have kept the faith!' we said;
   'We shall go down with reluctant tread
Rose-crowned into the darkness!' . . . Proud we were,
And laughed, that had such brave true things to say.
—And then you suddenly cried, and turned away.

1910

West Country

IVOR GURNEY

   Spring comes soon to Maisemore
      And spring comes sweet,
   With bird-songs and blue skies,
      On gay dancing feet;
   But she is such a sly lady
      I fear we'll never meet.

   Yet some day round a corner
      Where the hedge foams white,
   I'll find Spring sleeping
      In the young-crescent night,
   And seize her and make her
      Yield all her delight.

But yon's a glad story
   That's yet to be told.
Here's grey winter's bareness
   And no-shadowed cold.
O Spring, with your music,
   Your blue, green and gold,
Come shame his hard wisdom
   With laughter and gold!

Channel Firing

THOMAS HARDY

That night your great guns, unawares,
Shook all our coffins as we lay,
And broke the chancel window-squares,
We thought it was the Judgement-day

And sat upright. While drearisome
Arose the howl of awakened hounds:
The mouse let fall the altar-crumb,
The worm drew back into the mounds,

The glebe cow drooled. Till God called, 'No;
It's gunnery practice out at sea
Just as before you went below;
The world is as it used to be:

'All nations striving strong to make
Red war yet redder. Mad as hatters
They do no more for Christes sake
Than you who are helpless in such matters.

'That this is not the judgement-hour
For some of them's a blessed thing,

For if it were they'd have to scour
Hell's floor for so much threatening . . .

'Ha, ha! It will be warmer when
I blow the trumpet (if indeed
I ever do; for you are men,
And rest eternal sorely need).'

So down we lay again. 'I wonder,
Will the world ever saner be',
Said one, 'than when He sent us under
In our indifferent century!'

And many a skeleton shook his head.
'Instead of preaching forty year',
My neighbour Parson Thirdly said,
'I wish I had stuck to pipes and beer.'

Again the guns disturbed the hour,
Roaring their readiness to avenge,
So far inland as Stourton Tower,
And Camelot, and starlit Stonehenge.

April 1914

Epilogue

W. E. HENLEY

Into a land,
Storm-wrought, a place of quakes, all thunder-scarred,
Helpless, degraded, desolate,
Peace, the White Angel, comes.
Her eyes are as a mother's. Her good hands
Are comforting, and helping; and her voice

Falls on the Heart, as, after Winter, Spring
Falls on the World, and there is no more pain.
And in her influence, hope returns, and life,
And the passion of endeavour: so that, soon,
The idle ports are insolent with keels;
The stithies roar, and the mills thrum
With energy and achievement; weald and wold
Exult; the cottage-garden teems
With innocent hues and odours; boy and girl
Mate prosperously; there are sweet women to kiss;
There are good women to breed. In a golden fog,
A large, full-stomached faith in kindliness
All over the world, the nation, in a dream
Of money and love and sport, hangs at the paps
Of well-being, and so
Goes fattening, mellowing, dozing, rotting down
Into a rich deliquium* of decay.
Then if the Gods be good,
Then if the Gods be other than mischievous,
Down from their footstools, down
With a million-throated shouting, swoops and storms
War, the Red Angel, the Awakener,
The Shaker of Souls and Thrones; and at her heel
Trail grief, and ruin and shame!
The woman weeps her man, the mother her son,
The tenderling its father. In wild hours,
A people haggard with defeat,
Asks if there be a God; yet sets its teeth,
Faces calamity, and goes into the fire
Another than it was. And in wild hours,
A people, roaring ripe
With victory rises, menaces, stands renewed,
Sheds its piddling aims,
Approves its virtue, puts behind itself

* failure.

14

The comfortable dream, and goes,
Armoured and militant,
New-pithed, new souled, new visioned, up the steeps
To those great altitudes, whereat the weak
Live not but only the strong
Have leave to strive, and suffer, and achieve.

Vitai Lampada*

HENRY NEWBOLT

There's a breathless hush in the Close tonight—
    Ten to make and the match to win—
A bumping pitch and a blinding light,
    An hour to play and the last man in.
And it's not for the sake of a ribboned coat,
    Or the selfish hope of a season's fame,
But his Captain's hand on his shoulder smote:
    'Play up! play up! and play the game!'

The sand of the desert is sodden red,—
    Red with the wreck of a square† that broke;—
The Gatling's‡ jammed and the Colonel dead,
    And the regiment blind with dust and smoke,
The river of death has brimmed his banks,
    And England's far, and Honour a name,
But the voice of a schoolboy rallies the ranks:
    'Play up! play up! and play the game!'

This is the word that year by year,
    While in her place the School is set,
Every one of her sons must hear,
    And none that hears it dare forget.

* The Torch of Life, (school motto). † Corps of men. ‡ Gatling gun.

15

This they all with a joyful mind
   Beat through life like a torch in flame,
And falling fling to the host behind—
   'Play up! play up! and play the game!'

From My Diary, July 1914

WILFRED OWEN

Leaves
   Murmuring by myriads in the shimmering trees.
Lives
   Wakening with wonder in the Pyrenees.
Birds
   Cheerily chirping in the early day.
Bards
   Singing of summer, scything thro' the hay.
Bees
   Shaking the heavy dews from bloom and frond.
Boys
   Bursting the surface of the ebony pond.
Flashes
   Of swimmers carving thro' the sparkling cold.
Fleshes
   Gleaming with wetness to the morning gold.
A mead
   Bordered about with warbling water brooks.
A maid
   Laughing the love-laugh with me; proud of looks.
The heat
   Throbbing between the upland and the peak.
Her heart
   Quivering with passion to my pressèd cheek.
Braiding

Of floating flames across the mountain brow.
Brooding
Of stillness; and a sighing of the bough.
Stirs
Of leaflets in the gloom; soft petal-showers;
Stars
Expanding with the starr'd nocturnal flowers.

October

EDWARD THOMAS

The green elm with the one great bough of gold
Lets leaves into the grass slip, one by one,—
The short hill grass, the mushrooms small, milk-white,
Harebell and scabious and tormentil,
That blackberry and gorse, in dew and sun,
Bow down to; and the wind travels too light
To shake the fallen leaves from the fern;
The gossamers wander at their own will.
At heavier steps than birds' the squirrels scold.
The rich scene has grown fresh again and new
As Spring and to the touch is not more cool
Than it is warm to the gaze; and now I might
As happy be as earth is beautiful,
Were I some other or with earth could turn
In alternation of violet and rose,
Harebell and snowdrop, at their season due,
And gorse that has no time not to be gay.
But if this be not happiness,—who knows?
Some day I shall think this a happy day,
And this mood by the name of melancholy
Shall no more blackened and obscurèd be.

Reconciliation

WALT WHITMAN

Word over all, beautiful as the sky,
Beautiful that war and all its deeds of carnage must in time be
    utterly lost,
That the hands of the sisters Death and Night incessantly
    softly wash again, and ever again, this soil'd world;
For my enemy is dead, a man divine as myself is dead,
I look where he lies white-faced and still in the coffin—I draw
    near,
Bend down and touch lightly with my lips the white face in the
    coffin.

1865–6

A March in the Ranks Hard-Prest, and The Road Unknown

WALT WHITMAN

A march in the ranks hard-prest, and the road unknown,
A route through a heavy wood with muffled steps in the dark-
    ness,
Our army foil'd with loss severe, and the sullen remnant re-
    treating,
Till after midnight glimmer upon us the lights of a dim-lighted
    building,
We come to an open space in the woods, and halt by the dim-
    lighted building,
'Tis a large old church at the crossing roads, now an im-
    promptu hospital,
Entering but for a minute I see a sight beyond all the pictures
    and poems ever made,

Shadows of deepest, deepest black, just lit by moving candles
and lamps,
And by one great pitchy torch stationary with wild red flame
and clouds of smoke,
By these, crowds, groups of forms vaguely I see on the floor,
some in the pews laid down,
At my feet more distinctly a soldier, a mere lad, in danger of
bleeding to death, (he is shot in the abdomen,)
I stanch the blood temporarily, (the youngest face is as white as
a lily,)
Then before I depart, I sweep my eyes o'er the scene fain to
absorb it all,
Faces, varieties, postures beyond the description, most in
obscurity, some of them dead,
Surgeons operating, attendants holding lights, the smell of
ether, the odor of blood,
The crowd, O the crowd of the bloody forms, the yard outside
also fill'd,
Some on the bare ground, some on planks or stretchers, some
in death-spasm sweating,
An occasional scream or cry, the doctor's shouted orders or
calls,
The glisten of the little steel instruments catching the glint of
the torches,
These I resume as I chant, I see again the forms, I smell the
odor,
Them hear outside the orders given, *Fall in, my men, fall in*;
But first I bend to the dying lad, his eyes open, a half-smile gives
he me,
Then the eyes close, calmly close, and I speed forth to the dark-
ness,
Resuming, marching, even in darkness marching, on in the
ranks,
The unknown road still marching.

A Sight in Camp in the Daybreak Gray and Dim

WALT WHITMAN

A sight in the camp in the daybreak gray and dim,
As from my tent I emerge so early sleepless,
As slow I walk in the cool fresh air the path near by the hos-
pital tent,
Three forms I see on stretchers lying, brought out there un-
tended lying,
Over each the blanket spread, folding, covering all.

Curious I halt and silent stand,
Then with light fingers I from the face of the nearest the first
just lift the blanket;
Who are you elderly man so gaunt and grim, with well-gray'd
hair, and flesh all sunken about the eyes?
Who are you, my dear comrade?

Then to the second I step—and who are you, my child and
darling?
Who are you, sweet boy, with cheeks yet blooming?

Then to the third—a face nor child nor old, very calm, as of
beautiful yellow-white ivory;
Young man I think I know you—I think this face is the face of
the Christ himself,
Dead and divine and brother of all, and here again he lies.

2 Marching

'Sorley's Weather'

One hundred pages of poetry reveal many changes in both style and outlook. Where in 1914 and 1915 war was thought to be a purifier in its effects upon combatants, a therapeutic or a toughener of the moral fibre, the lyric form was adequate. A poet could well *sing* the sentiments of William Watson or Rupert Brooke, and any overtones caught from the nineteenth century were advantageous. But once the total attitude changed it would have been better to renounce the lyric for a more philosophical medium, to abandon stanzaic movement for blank or free verse such as had been discovered at the opening of the century but was not developed more extensively until after the war. Where in 1916 and onwards war becomes a brutalising agent and the soldier a degraded patient driven into a hell of insanity, hysteria and cowardice, it invites ridicule to sing of it in lyrical measures. Only Isaac Rosenberg—always the odd man out—attempted the ambitious dramatic form in the trenches, while the epic, like the novel, was beyond the power of a fighter in the middle of a war. The novels and prose books of the war are characteristic of the 1920s when time for concentration was available. The great majority of writers, indeed, took lyrical forms from their romantic heritage, but it is most of all when they used them ironically that they achieved notable expression.

The 1914 crop of poetry, being anterior to battle experience, has been spoken of already. The 'boys' did not come back for Christmas and in 1915 it became evident that they would not be at home that year either. The Western Front became an irremovable deadlock and the only means to continue hostilities was to sidestep it. Thus in 1915 began expeditions to Gallipoli and Salonika, which were doomed to failure, as ways of forcing a back-door attack upon Germany and an onslaught upon the Turks.

In that year, too, came the death of RUPERT BROOKE at sea

on his way to a naval engagement in the Aegean waters. His sonnets written in 1914 had made him famous, but his death produced an apotheosis. The young golden-haired Apollo was admired by multitudes. D. H. Lawrence found him 'a Greek god under a Japanese sunshade' at his home near Cambridge, and Winston Churchill commended his poems. Dean Inge quoted them from Westminster pulpit, for who can deny that they spoke to England of its place in the world? The modern reader may find them embarrassing and chauvinistic, but he must accept them as seminal pieces which did a great deal to win the public for war poetry. Without Brooke's sonnets, which do not represent the best of his abilities, there might have been fewer poems from other men and poetry might not have become the dominant wartime art form for the young. If he was there as a subject for elegies, none of them much more than routine work, Brooke was also there for others to criticize and against whom to measure their own waning ideals. A new reader is advised to glance at them with clear eyes and assess them entirely for himself.

One must always link JULIAN GRENFELL with Rupert Brooke, since he was a writer of the same idealistic school. In 1914 he wrote in a letter: 'I adore War. It is like a big picnic without the objectlessness of a picnic.' In the next year he composed his best poem 'Into Battle'. There he went further and said:

> And he is dead who will not fight
> And who dies fighting has increase.

The lyricism of the poem does not persuade the critic to accept all the implications of the word 'increase', but as a document in the history of poetry which is also closely allied to the history of taste he should be aware of the comment published by a contemporary, the anthologist, E. B. Osborn. He wrote of 'Into Battle' as being 'a vindication of war as a mode of intense living, harmonious with the deepest nature of man in which all sham emotions and rootless thoughts and sick sophistries are consumed as in a refiner's fire'. It is a representative modern verdict that the attitudes conveyed and sung in 'Into Battle' are the sham ones, but in Grenfell's day it was not understood so.

Robert Graves wrote a poem in memory of another dead poet, CHARLES HAMILTON SORLEY, with the title that stands at the head of this section. I have appropriated that title for the changing mood of 1915 when there remained a moderate optimism, with only a limited dissatisfaction at the conduct of the war. The turning-point was still out of sight.

But as a preface we should turn to a poem by D. H. Lawrence, a civilian. When war broke out he was on a walking tour in the Lake District and the news was slow to reach him. His reaction was violent. He wrote in one of his letters, many of which belong to war literature, that his 'soul lay in the tomb, but with a flat stone over it, a corpse, become corpse-cold'. In 1915 he was stating in free verse:

> We have gone too far, oh very much too far.
> Only attend to the noiseless multitudes
> Of ghosts that throng about our muddled hearts.

Charles Sorley, a good deal younger, hadn't the colloquial freedom of Lawrence at his best. One finds romantic rhetoric again, though the heart is changing:

> When you see millions of the mouthless dead
> Across your dreams in pale battalions go,
> Say not soft things as other men have said,
> That you'll remember. For you need not so.

There is a pronounced echo of Keats in line three; the 'other men' are those who wrote in Brooke's weather. Sorley thought very hard about the state of Europe, having visited Germany shortly before the fatal August, and gave consideration to some of the diplomatic problems of reconciliation:

> But until peace, the storm,
> The darkness and the thunder and the rain.

Since he was twenty at the time of his death, an allowance for technical immaturity has to be made, as it has for all who were killed before they could develop their verbal art. In attitude the poem strikes independent ground. Would Sorley have become a poet or diplomat, one wonders, if he had returned? His father was a Cambridge professor, and it is not irrelevant to note that his surviving cousin is Lord Butler, formerly the Tory politician, R. A. Butler. What poetry we have lost by the sudden deaths of writers we can but speculate upon, as we have pondered the premature deaths of Keats, Shelley and Byron. Sorley's political understanding opens a distinct line of conjecture:

did England suffer after 1945 from the scarcity of politicians resulting from the high mortality on the Western Front? This was when their presence would have been most valuable.

Oxford and Cambridge war poets abound, though Sorley gives the impression of being their superior. There is, in fact, a depressing sameness about them all: a little public school poetry (Sorley wrote at Marlborough) and a few university pieces, a handful written during initial corps training and finally a series of combat reflections. The whole collection would be pieced together perhaps by a college tutor who could do little but mourn the man's death and communicate some of his sense of bitter regret. As representative, I have chosen WILLIAM NOEL HODGSON from Oxford. A great admirer of Rupert Brooke, he wrote poetry that shows much greater strain than anything his hero was called upon to undergo. The rhythm in this extract is far from subtle, but the images, with their clear religious connotations, attempt to render the terror of a man barely able to maintain poise in the face of it:

> We that have seen the strongest
> Cry like a beaten child,
> The sanest eyes unholy,
> The cleanest hands defiled,
> We that have known the heart blood
> Less than the lees of wine,
> We that have seen man broken
> We know that man is divine.

The critic will undoubtedly point to the unrealised imagery of the 'lees of wine', but he may see in it an honesty and a departure from the old confidence of the soldier offering up hands undefiled on his deathbed. If the poem Hodgson wrote two days before his death is read immediately after this one, his acceptance of the Christian faith is found to have grown more perfect. The historian is led to comment on an aspect of war poetry: how little religious conviction there is in the poetry of the closing years of the war. Wilfred Owen uses images from the Bible as points of departure and reservoirs of traditional wisdom ironically to show that human behaviour offers nothing but a rejection of tradition. Graves once remarked that 'there was no patriotism in the trenches'; indeed, how much religion remained when the optimism of 1914 was played out?

An older writer than Sorley whose poetry shares a similar honesty is EDWARD THOMAS. War poetry is not his true medium, but in 'The Trumpet' there is the artistic integrity and self-knowledge that is so impressive in his best pastoral poems. He understands that to yield to sleep at the call of the trumpet is a metaphor for yielding to thoughts of annihilation:

> Here love ends,
> Despair, ambition ends;
> All pleasure and all trouble.

He notes:

> I must enter, and leave, alone,
> I know not how.

His friends say that Thomas contrived to enjoy the rituals of army life: there is at least no protest. It is as if he accepted his fate and deliberately acquired a new point of mental balance. Even if it may look Brookean torn out of context, this passage is devoid of Georgian wistfulness. The rhythm alone shows that the stanza is being consciously and ironically used:

> Nobody knows but God,
> Whether I am destined to lie
> Under a foreign clod.

Thomas remained the sensitive and subtle intelligence until his death in action. His early life made him a countryman and one reads his poem 'A Private' as a piece of self-identification with the dead ploughman:

> And where now at last he sleeps
> More sound in France—that, too, he secret keeps.

This section closes appropriately with Thomas. Even if his life took him over the turning-point of the war, his poetry remains at the stage in which romanticism has been forced away and with complete integrity the poet takes stock of the war.

Turning-points—from 1916

Poems have to be drafted, polished and revised, a process sometimes taking months. It is common to have them published in a magazine and then, at a later date, to revise them in a one-man volume. In the process years may elapse and the poet may no longer own that small portion of his thought that went into the making of a few precise lines. We should bear in mind that a trench poet was likely to alter his concept more quickly than a Georgian, and that to him delayed publication would be particularly unfair. So it is that the historian of a fast-developing situation like the Great War is likely to remain inaccurate in chronology. The clubmen and the clerics at home, like the oft-published Canon Rawnsley, were quite unaware of many developments. Long after the armistice there were readers who considered the literature of protest and pacifism as an aberration, only worthy of suppression.

There seems little doubt that the turning-point in the war occurred about the year 1916. It was the year of the Battle of the Somme. The Liberal government was defeated after a crisis in the munitions industry and a great rise in prices. The national hero, Lord Kitchener, was drowned in *H.M.S. Hampshire*, a tragedy that many thought was engineered by personal enemies. His disappearance resulted in the ascendancy of the most controversial of all war leaders, Douglas Haig, and heralded the introduction of conscription for war service, since the original force from voluntary service was inadequate to keep pace with the slaughter.

Nineteen hundred and sixteen was also the year of the Easter Rising in Dublin, a decisive act of self-assertion by the southern Irish which led towards their ultimate independence. The unquestioned master of Irish poetry, W. B. Yeats, like all his compatriots, was too engrossed in the emergence of the Irish nation to write poetry upon the conflict between England and Germany. His 'Irish Airman Foresees his Death' is not included in this volume since its place is elsewhere. One might equally well include 'Leda and the Swan' or 'The Second Coming': the reader will need no prompting to turn to Yeats as the most significant poet of his generation. The Irish writer Francis Ledwidge, who fought in British armies, is included. He was so much an individual, a leprechaun-haunted Celt, that one is not surprised to find him inattentive to the demands of war discipline. Ireland has, throughout this century, remained deep in its own mythology and political history so that its literature is largely estranged from our own.

James Joyce's comic and independent piece on p. 82 is a characteristic neutral joke.

With Field Marshal Haig in command it was not long before the poetic voice was at last raised in protest. Sir Henry Newbolt, it is not too difficult to foresee, admired Haig, but Robert Graves and Siegfried Sassoon, as well as many high-ranking officers, repudiated his contempt for human life. Especially culpable was the choice of the fields of Flanders for an autumn encounter in 1917 when rain, mud and cold were almost as deadly as the Germans. In excuse of the conditions so horrifically realised by Herbert Read on p. 109, Haig stated that there 'was no reason to anticipate the heavy rainfall'.

If there is one historical study that is likely to appeal to the reader of war literature it is *In Flanders Fields* by Leon Wolff. In it the horrors of the campaign reach a vividness that cannot easily be forgotten. Haig, the founder of Poppy Day, appears there in monstrous proportions, and his most recent biographer, John Terraine, who claimed the Field Marshal as a cultured soldier, completely fails to exonerate him. For one brief, almost nonchalant, ironic poem on Haig there is Siegfried Sassoon's 'The General' in which his indifference to the fate of his own men is smartly hit off:

> But he did for them both with his plan of attack.

Though militarists were slow to see it, some poets recognized 1916 as the turning point of the war. There is, for a start, the book *Battle*, by WILFRID WILSON GIBSON, published in that year, which is outstanding for its violence. Gibson himself saw very little fighting and it is impossible to judge whether his poems were based upon experience or not. One suspects that they were not. If that is the case, he was a civilian of intense dramatic vision, for whom the terrors of war were active in his mind and would not, in Keats's phrase, 'let him rest'. His poem 'In the Ambulance' is highly charged journalism, but it heralds the poetry of sharp protest which is properly the writer's province:

> Both his legs are shot away,
> And his head is light,
> So he keeps on muttering
> All the blessed night.

In later years, when Siegfried Sassoon was especially noted for the poetry of irony and violence, Gibson's touch deserted him. His inverted poetic development suggests that he had experienced too little to write at that pitch continuously and his later poems show a writer who had begun to lose contact.

The early poems of the *Battle* volume come as a surprise to readers who associate Gibson with 'Flannan Isle' or his Georgian books. Similarly, it is the Kipling of the disillusioned poems on pp. 85–6 (written after the death of his son) who is still read, though as the author of such patriotic pieces as 'Recessional' he is dismissed by some people as no better than a hypocrite.

From A. G. West to Herbert Read

Hereafter, space does not permit us to consider the conservative, cautious voices of many opinions from the nation at home. At this point we turn to two poems by ARTHUR GRAEME WEST, a writer who remains largely unfamiliar. Like Sorley he devoted his time to demolishing the legends of chivalric war:

> God! how I hate you, you young cheerful men,
> Whose pious poetry blossoms on your graves
> As soon as you are in them.

He enumerates some current platitudes:

> How rare life is!
> On earth, the love and fellowship of men,
> Men sternly banded: banded for what end?
> Banded to maim and kill their fellow men—
> For even Huns are men. In Heaven above
> A genial umpire, a good Judge of sport
> Won't let us hurt each other.

His was a sensibility that moved swiftly towards atheism. It was also precise:

> His head
> Smashed like an eggshell and the warm grey brain
> Spattered all bloody.

And in 'The Night Patrol' the outlook is at first almost botanical:

> . . . tufts of crackling cornstalks, two years old,
> No man had reaped, and patches of spring grass.

where he comes upon this startling scene:

> The slimy pools—the dead man stank through all,
> Pungent and sharp.

This poem is one of the masterpieces of the genre of protest, powerful beyond anything written by Sorley. A lyric metre— it will be seen—has been discarded in favour of the medium of blank verse. On the evidence of such poems one is inclined to predict quite as much for West's hypothetical future as for Sorley's.

The next group of writers is of those who survived longest to preserve the correct understanding of comrades who died. EDMUND BLUNDEN has always been pre-eminent in this undertaking and particularly tireless in introducing readers to the entire range of war writers, once known or unknown to him. His own war poetry shows, again, the perception of an amateur botanist sharpened to a pitch of visual artistry and refinement:

> Ember-black the gibbet trees like bones or thorns
>   protrude
> From the poisonous smoke   past all impulses.

Blunden's images of destructiveness are used as moral comment. In this respect he resembles nobody so much as the artist Paul Nash, whose autobiography *Outline* contains similar impressions: 'The stinking mud becomes more evilly yellow, the shell holes full up with green-white water . . . the black dying trees ooze and sweat and the shells never cease.' And in this connection one recalls the pleading of the Duke of Burgundy for the land of France in a war 500 years earlier in Shakespeare's *Henry V*:

> The even mead, that erst brought sweetly forth
> The freckled cowslip, burnet and green clover,
> Wanting the scythe, all uncorrected, rank,
> Conceives by idleness, and nothing teems

> But hateful docks, rough thistles, kecksies, burs,
> Losing both beauty and utility.

In *Henry IV* one swiftly comes to recognise Hotspur's, Hal's and Falstaff's distinct attitudes to military prowess and glory. In the poems that disclose the ruin of nature lies the Burgundy attitude to warfare, which is also a moral attitude. Blunden's familiar 'Report on Experience' inspects the ravaged land itself in his threefold conception, together with the image of righteousness forsaken and chastity reduced to prostitution.

In 'Zero' Blunden takes his moral attitude to warfare further, virtually doubting the continuance of divine providence: 'Has the old cosmic fire grown tame?'—a question similar to Wilfred Owen's unforgettable: 'Was it for this the clay grew tall?' But, in general, Blunden's muse is not a pessimistic one, stoic perhaps: 'It's plain we were born for this, naught else.' Sorley expressed the same note in his 'So be merry, so be dead'.

Nevertheless, Blunden felt himself visited by a muse. As late as 1916 he could still write of elves and pixies under a stone while Graves published a book with the rather embarrassing title, 'Fairies and Fusiliers'. Each of them had a long way to travel before 1918. We meet Blunden once more in the third section of this anthology where he is again in a garden setting: 'Mellow between the leafy maze smiles down/September's sun.' It is the same 'fantastic garden' as he sought in respite from battle. His verse, always rich and specific in sensory detail, seems to have been a way of keeping a grip, or reassuring himself that there was something left to return to when he was demobilised. At this point he returns to his thoughts about his wartime experiences, with the implicit message, 'Look, we have come through'.

ROBERT GRAVES would deserve full treatment here if he had not preferred to suppress most of his early poetry and refuse permission for its reprinting. We are fortunate in having his fine autobiography, *Goodbye to All That*. It shares with Blunden's *Undertones of War* and Sassoon's *Journal of an Infantry Officer* the highest position among the prose interpretations of the war years. It might be noted, however, that G. S. Fraser has called Blunden's book his best war *poem* and has even printed an extract from it in *The London Magazine* in free verse. The two Graves poems which are reprinted demand the backing of his autobiography. Readers will find the war chapters from both these prose accounts contrasted and reprinted in Douglas Brown's *A Book of Modern Prose*.

For long a survivor was SIEGFRIED SASSOON, a member of the Georgian group. He too found his early heroic war poems embarrassing in their idealism since he was so slow to react against the wastefulness of the war and turn to pacifism. In danger of court-martial for his opinions, he was taken instead to Craiglockhart in Scotland, a hospital which treated cases of shellshock. Removed for a time from the front line a momentous meeting was prepared for him with another poet among the patients, a reader of Sassoon's writings, named Wilfred Owen.

All the truly characteristic Sassoon work aims at the exposure of cant and hypocrisy. His blend of dialogue with its succinct moralisation leaves the reader in no doubt; his poetry is extremely easy to assimilate, though the occasional lack of subtlety has the effect of dulling the reader's receptiveness—as in this scene:

'God blast your neck!' (For days he'd had no sleep)
'Get up and guide me through this stinking place.'
Savage he kicked a soft unanswering heap,
And flashed his beam across the livid face
Terribly glaring up, whose eyes yet wore
Agony dying hard ten days before.

Sassoon's parenthesis in the first line is revealing. After such knowledge many individuals would have found self-command impossible:

Feebly now he drags
Exhausted ego back from glooms and quags
And blasting tumult, terror, hurtling glare,
To calm and brightness, havens of sweet air.

The critic Middleton Murry diagnosed the lack of subtlety and control in Sassoon's poetry in this sentence: 'An inhuman experience can only be rightly rendered by rendering also its relation to the harmony of the soul it shatters.' For many pages Sassoon provides no positive strength, leaving only the deadening impact upon the reader's nerves equivalent to the strain and hysteria the experiences brought to his own. Yet by so doing he gave his poetry great immediacy.

The only literary model that Sassoon acknowledged was Thomas Hardy's *Satires of Circumstance* which expose the harshness of fate in a like way. By the time Sassoon published his *Counter-Attack* he had communicated his opinions to a wide circle of readers. In the process he vindicated any initial unpopularity by his compassionate studies of the circumstances of the fighting men. So overwhelming a sense of disillusion as his could not be silenced at the end of the war. At first, he returned to write of the scenes of battle in peacetime and then to question what had been bought with the immense losses. Later still, following a fallow period, he found postwar topics for what was now his naturally satirical insight.

Very close in spirit to Sassoon's is some of the poetry of HERBERT READ. He conveys the close paternalistic relations of officer to his men in 'My Company'. He also sounds a vein of dark satire. Nowhere in the literature of the war is the horror of campaigning through the mud in Flanders more dramatically caught in words:

> He clutched and they tugged,
> But slowly he sank.
> His terror grew—
> Grew visibly when the viscous ooze
> Reached his neck . . .
> An officer shot him through the head.

Who knows how often a young officer was faced with such a task or, for that matter, how many men were sent to the firing squad for attempted mutiny and desertion during the later stages of the war? The after-effect of reading such poetry is, however, that one grows immune when the nakedness of the experience is there untransmuted.

This bareness is all the more remarkable in view of the fact that Read was at the same time a member of the group of English writers who were influenced by the Imagist school of poets formed by some Americans. These included Ezra Pound, Amy Lowell and Hilda Doolittle. Proceeding from a manifesto which demanded above all brevity and concentration in a poem, they expected that imagery should be the emotional focus. After a period the writers quarrelled over first principles and split up. There are not many Imagist poems on the war. Read's 'Ypres' is an example.

In a sense an economical Imagist poem is 'open-ended' in that the reader is invited to complete the meaning of the picture from his own experience and to supply his own moral comment. It is a criticism of many such poems that they lack the compelling movement that binds a poem together and degenerate into rhythmical inertness precisely because of the concentration upon imagery alone.

Richard Aldington, D. H. Lawrence and Ford Madox Ford were three other English Imagists who wrote upon war topics. Aldington's attractively naïve 'Soliloquy I' has no apparent connection with the movement:

> No I'm not afraid of death
> (Not very much afraid, that is)

D. H. Lawrence is sometimes a practising Imagist in his war poems and there is a hint of this same technique in the work of Rosenberg.

Amongst Herbert Read's studies of men at the end of their tether, we have his imitation of Wordsworth's 'Happy Warrior'. The nineteenth-century original is in an eighteenth-century manner, abstract nouns and personifications hiding force of emotion:

> doomed to go in company with Pain,
> And Fear, and Bloodshed, miserable train,
> Turns his necessity to glorious gain,

Read's revision is totally different:

> He cannot shriek.
> Bloody saliva
> Dribbles down his shapeless jacket.

It is particularly appropriate that this section be concluded with the work of EDGELL RICKWORD, who was like Herbert Read in bringing a much wider literary culture to the task of writing war poetry. He knew, apparently, the works of Rilke and Rimbaud and went on to publish a study of the latter. Two lines from his 'Trench Poets' stand at the head of this volume as the complete antithesis of Ivor Gurney's heroic rhetoric. Still more impressive than that piece of black comedy is the poem 'The Soldier addresses his Body' which has a freshness of sensation that makes Georgian poetry seem parochial.

For Rickword youth is a time for the amassing of great knowledge and experience:

> Yet there's a world of things we haven't done,
> countries not seen, where people do strange things.

He turns from that strangeness to the legendary and fabulous beasts and proposes a much wider education through travel:

> Vodka and kvass and bitter mountain wines
> we've never drunk, nor snatched at bursting grapes
> to pelt slim girls among Sicilian vines.

I would give many pages of other writers for that last image. It reminds us how rare is an appreciation of a young woman's part in a man's experience as it is depicted in war poetry, where the presiding emotions are the preservation of life and the exploitation of comradeship. Many poets seem quite nonsexual, offering occasionally the shadowy image of mother, wife or sweetheart who are unreal intrusions into the reflections of a man's world. We recall the criticism by T. S. Eliot on public school sentiments quoted on p. 4.

At the end of 'The Soldier addresses his Body' he turns to it with the peculiar self-directed irony that is so successful in the modern poems by Philip Larkin: 'let's have a drink and give the cards a run.' This way of postponing reflections and mature decisions is in no sense a rejection of responsibility and one senses that Mr Rickword was a satirically-minded and unsentimental soldier with an alert sensibility and intelligence.

While the reader feels an empathy for a creative writer who needed the open air of the countryside to help him retain his grip on life, he may also regret that it resulted in nothing more exotic than an image of the British travel poster rustic lane. Such writing is the result of restricting and foreshortening valuable experience and leads in the end to insularity—and this amongst a group of Englishmen who most needed to be explorers. There are, after all, more colourful stimuli to creativity than nostalgia and there have been many writers for whom a bohemian life has been beneficial. W. B. Yeats remarked drily that he had known more artists ruined by a good wife and children than by dissolute company. The aesthetes of the 1890s, drug-takers and perverts, all became respectable in the end and often joined the Roman Catholic Church, but the Georgians seemed to have lived whole lives cut off from vital forms of excitement.

After Edgell Rickword and Herbert Read we are likely to be less enthusiastic about many of their contemporaries, though we accept the advantages both Georgians and Trench Poets had from the support of a determined readership. We may understand this better if we consider the 1920s. Before 1914 it was possible for the reader to have sampled the early writings of T. S. Eliot, Ezra Pound, Marcel Proust and James Joyce, who were all publishing their first books from about 1910 onwards. Thinkers such as Marx, Freud, Jung and Fraser, became immensely influential in many countries after the war, but were all accessible by 1914. Psychology and anthropology, especially, became essential insights for those who sought to express the nature of man in twentieth-century terms. It was also, to take other art forms, possible before the war for the post-impressionist painters, the Diaghilev ballets and the Beecham operatic seasons to transform the conventional English ideas of art. Whatever influence these manifestations had in later years, they remained outside the mental world of most war poets.

After the war one supposes that the work of Joyce, Eliot, Pound, and Lawrence drew increasing attention to that of Freud, Jung, Fraser and Karl Marx. Herbert Read, writing in 1925, however, still criticised English writers for failing to find verbal forms adapted to modern ways of thinking and feeling. 'There is', he wrote in an essay on 'The Future of Poetry', 'no adequate literary equivalent in England for the impressive organisation and intellectual content of the modern movement in painting.'

War poetry held its public because it was little short of one's duty to attend to it. There has been no sizeable audience for poetry since. John Betjeman and Dylan Thomas, in their different ways, have acquired considerable fame, but the poets in the 1930s wrote for a very limited range of reader, and much subsequent work appears to have been published principally for other poets, critics and dons. From the viewpoint of the highly educated reader the intellectual range of most trench poets is unimpressive and modern critics have at times dismissed virtually all war writers, idealists and protesters alike, as great disappointments. One reviewer, P. N. Furbank, writing in *The*

Guardian in 1965 is typical: 'I can see no consequences flowing from the Great War poets; and only, perhaps a minor achievement. Some very poignant but flawed poems by Wilfred Owen, two or three poems of remarkable power . . . by Isaac Rosenberg.'

The reader is invited to consider his verdict. If he rejects this view, he will not need to make defences for the poets; if he accepts it he will find an explanation in the outlook and education of prewar England and may wonder whether and in what ways the cultural state of the country at the present time is different. In either case he is bound to find innumerable comparisons and contrasts through the anthology with which to refine his critical sense.

Waiting for the End: Owen and Rosenberg

The year 1917 was marked by the outbreak of the Russian Revolution and the consequent withdrawal of Russian armies from the Allied forces. The long-delayed entry of America went some of the way to filling that gap by making fresh detachments available for the Western Front. Even in 1918 there was no guarantee of an Allied victory and the success of the German submarine attacks on shipping in the Atlantic forced Britain to introduce food-rationing for the first time. It may have looked to the German Command as if they could starve their enemies out, but the final attack on Mons by Douglas Haig brought the war to a halt at last on 11 November 1918. The Armistice had been so long coming that there was unrestrained revelry throughout England when the news was released, though all the minor pockets of war in the Near East had not been mopped up when hostilities ended on the Western Front.

One of the ironies of this final stage for the reader of English literature is that if the war could have ended one week sooner, WILFRED OWEN would not have perished. The poems found in his notebooks were printed in 1920 with the editorial collaboration of Siegfried Sassoon and Osbert Sitwell. Their qualities were not immediately noticed for it was not until the 1940s that they circulated in great numbers. In 1934, indeed, a writer in *The Army Quarterly* looked back over twenty years and still singled out Rupert Brooke and Julian Grenfell, dismissing as dangerously unbalanced some unnamed writers who attacked the war or the peace settlement of 1919. Yet it was at about this time that younger poets discovered Owen's technical achievements and his unmatched compassion for his whole doomed generation. The technical device of pararhyme in which words are coupled on their consonant structure alone instead of their vowel sounds was held to be a great extension of poetic technique. One poet, Patric Dickinson, has recorded in his recent autobiography, *The Good Minute*, his great devotion to the poetry of Owen before the outbreak of the Second World War. Had Owen survived the battle—such is the capriciousness of taste—it is probable that he would not be so self-evidently the writer whom all critics single out for praise.

The use by Benjamin Britten of a sequence of Owen's poems for the solo arias in his *War Requiem* of 1962 has made still more people acquainted with them. An American music critic remarked in 1963 that Owen and Britten had become an article of faith among liberally-minded English people. The *War Requiem* takes for its first solo 'Anthem for Doomed Youth', one that is especially apt for musical setting. In it the poet imagines a whole generation slaughtered and it is the sort of poem, as a critic has remarked, that Brooke himself might have written if he had lived longer:

> Not in the hands of boys, but in their eyes
> Shall shine the holy glimmers of good-byes.

We learn to expect unevenness in Owen's work. More characteristic of his best writing is his use of mythological figures such as Abraham who becomes the symbol of the old man who sacrifices the young one Isaac, and 'half the seed of Europe one by one'.

It is also possible to find traces of Shelley and Keats in Owen. His literary education did not include the Metaphysicals or much foreign poetry, apart from a certain quantity of French verse that he read during his stay in the country before the outbreak of the war. Any collector of Romantic phrases must recognise the source of some in this extract from 'Strange Meeting':

> I went hunting wild
> After the *wildest beauty* in the world,
> Which lies not *calm* in eyes, or *braided hair*,

> But mocks the steady running of the hour,
> And if it grieves, *grieves richlier* than here.

That poem exerts a special fascination because of the originality of its scenario, a meeting between two dead soldiers in Hell.
It may recall Dante's *Inferno* or a German Expressionist film or
painting with two figures, once enemies, now only persons
face to face: 'I am the enemy you killed, my friend.' The note of
fraternization and compassion in the midst of battle is that
which is most admirable in Owen's sensibility.

For living poets such as W. H. Auden it may be Owen's
blend of Romanticism and colloquialism that has proved as
attractive as his extension of rhyming techniques. The jaunti-
ness of this next extract creates an unheroic tone most welcome
to those who value the presence of irony in a poem:

> Out there we've walked quite friendly up to Death;
> Sat down and eaten with him, cool and bland,
> Pardoned his spilling mess-tins in our hand.
> We've sniffed the green thick odour of his breath.

Owen appears today as the writer who commands images of
damnation, like the French *poètes maudits* (outcast poets) of the
late nineteenth century, placing them not in a seething background of town life as in Baudelaire but transplanted to the
battlefield: 'the blood/Come gargling from the froth-corrupted
lungs.'

He can admittedly sometimes fumble for words, put word
over word with an arbitrariness that reminds us that many of
the poems are unfinished. Even 'Strange Meeting' is not fully
realised:

> They will be swift with the swiftness of the tigress,
> None will break ranks, though nations trek from progress.
> Courage was mine and I had mystery
> Wisdom was mine, and I had mastery,

The words *courage* and *wisdom*, *mystery* and *mastery* here could be
interchanged without distinct loss and the feminine para-
rhymes here (rhymes on double syllables) do not save the
expression from artificiality. In the phrase 'trek from progress'
it is difficult to justify the unusual first word when in no
instance can *progress* ever be a starting point.

Finally, however, it is generally admitted that Owen's was

an impressive attempt to penetrate the mystery of war and find the common humanity that opponents share. For many, Owen goes further to see in war a metaphor for the precariousness of all human effort. Such a view of human history gives greater poignancy to his outstandingly successful line, an elegy for all generations: 'Was it for this that clay grew tall?'

With ISAAC ROSENBERG we reach a man who was an artist as well as a poet, one with a completely fresh set of attitudes and interests. He was the trench poet who was most perfectly detached from the war. In spite of the inevitable discomforts he nowhere complains, and it would seem from his writing that he was in the trenches, avid for experience, partly to earn a separation allowance for his mother.

Had he not existed, nobody could have invented a Rosenberg in the thick of the mud, the rifle-fire and the marching feet. The Imagist in him speaks in his early poetry:

> Three lives hath one life—
> Iron, honey, gold.
> The gold, the honey gone—
> Left is the hard and cold.

He submerges himself in a detachment of marchers and takes over their rhythm in his prosody:

> Like flaming pendulums, hands
> Swing across the khaki—
> Mustard-coloured khaki—
> To the automatic feet.

Such sound effects are as the vivid sense of human life in the barrack-room picture of his companions looking for lice in their shirts:

> Nudes, stark and glistening,
> Yelling in lurid glee. Grinning faces
> All raging limbs
> Whirl over the floor on fire.

The effect is that of the frozen music of sculpture. The writer never asks such questions as Why am I fighting? Should men be reduced to automatic feet? He seems to have been perfectly equipped to write the most elaborate allegories and dramatic scenes based upon Hebrew mythology while he was fighting.

His only problems were the aesthetic ones: what verbal colours and images will be most appropriate to convey all this experience?

Rosenberg can suggest the penetrating vision of William Blake:

> I saw in prophetic gleams
> These mighty daughters in their dances
> Beckon each soul aghast from its crimson corpse
> To mix in their glittering dances.

'Dead Man's Dump' is his most horrific poem, though 'Break of Day in the Trenches' with its ironical self-portrait ('The parapet's poppy behind my ear') possesses something equally original. Its subsidiary hero is a 'sardonic rat' who is made the viewpoint of the whole scene. In this respect he is like the 'casual tramp' in Owen's 'The Send-Off', one of his best poems, which makes play with lines of contrasting length. For Rosenberg the rat is both the observer and the indifferent one who can pass without favour from German to English trenches with the 'cosmopolitan sympathies' that these two distinguished trench poets shared with an initially small audience.

The delay in Rosenberg's acceptance by the public must spring from a dislike for the man who sits upon the fence. We accept a world view in which there must always be two camps, and philosophical neutrality, difficult to attain, will always be subject to criticism from the partisan. It will probably be admitted that Rosenberg left further difficulties for his reader by imposing so much strain upon words and imagery. It was his aim to be ambiguous and, in his own words, 'understandable and still ungraspable': concepts that we are more likely to expect from poets of the 1920s (from Eliot or William Empson in particular), whose works are often capable of communicating to the reader before they are fully understood.

It is a common opinion that Rosenberg's work must inevitably be judged the more individual and remarkable. For remoteness and originality only Owen's 'Strange Meeting' can be compared. Although it cannot be said to be a widely held view, some critical opinion does regard Rosenberg as the greatest writer of the entire group, comparable with those of far greater literary culture than himself for his submission to the life of the trenches and the harvest he reaped from it. But he was one who had no dealings with the rustic muse and found the torture of his own generation a subject for calm appraisal.

Two Civilian Poets

Throughout the war there were always bystanders who formed the audience for all that was best in war poetry. There were many, on the other hand, whose obtuseness reflected no credit upon their society. Of the latter category one might single out Alice Meynell, on the showing of her contribution to this book.

For doggerel which represents what a large number of people were thinking one can turn to the works in verse and prose of the Rev. Studdert-Kennedy, known as 'Woodbine Willie'; or, a rarer case, the poems and recitation entertainments, complete with lantern-slides, of Mackenzie Bell. The curiosity printed on p. 45 represents our nadir, suggesting that the British people, always animal lovers, thought that the treatment of old horses was a matter fit for wartime verse.

Two civilian poets who expressed the sentiments of 1918 conclude this discussion. LAURENCE BINYON's 'For the Fallen' is always associated with the ceremony at the Cenotaph on 11 November, although it was written much earlier. His lines have the rhythms of the Bible and contain a submerged quotation from *Antony and Cleopatra* ('Age cannot wither her'):

> They shall not grow old, as we that are left grow old:
> Age shall not weary them, nor the years condemn.
> At the going down of the sun and in the morning
> We will remember them.

A parallel comes from another civilian poem, *Prufrock* by T.S. Eliot, written in the same year. There his anti-hero remarks ironically:

> I grow old . . . I grow old
> I shall wear the bottoms of my trousers rolled.

The resemblance is probably coincidental: there could hardly be greater contrast.

The second voice in this closing section comes from an age-ing writer whose reputation has markedly increased. THOMAS

HARDY was over seventy at the outbreak of the war and could think back through several European wars as well as colonial engagements. In 'Before Marching and After' he employs a technique common in his poetry: mingling past and present and evaluating what is new from his long-maturing judgment. 'And there was a great calm', written in November 1918, is the finest of all his comments on war. At first, the past is conveyed in a series of personifications which are distanced and kept outside the field of experience:

> There had been years of Passion—scorching, cold,
> And much Despair, and Anger heaving high,
> Care whitely watching, Sorrows manifold.

Upon this the writer lets loose quite different language for the next stage of history:

> 'Hell!' and 'Shell!' were yapped at Loving-kindness.

The words then create a fresh series of national experiences:

> The feeble folk at home had grown full-used
> To 'dug-outs', 'snipers', 'Huns' from the war-adept.

Though they were *full-used* the inverted commas are intended to tell us that they had nevertheless failed to understand what such words meant.

The climax of the poem is the calm of the armistice with the economical movement of words adding greatly to the theme:

> Aye; all was hushed. The about-to fire fired not,
> The aimed-at moved away in a trance-lipped song.

In Hardy's poetry there is often a cumbersome quality, an archaism in the use of language. That is the case here yet, it catches precisely a moment which stands outside time, the original two minutes' silence.

The poem ends with the view of Olympian observers, spirits gifted with Hardy's own viewpoint:

> The Sinister Spirit sneered, 'It had to be!'
> And again the Spirit of Pity whispered 'Why?'

In both its subject-matter and its command of language it sums up the English poet's journey from August 1914 to November 1918.

In the Trenches

RICHARD ALDINGTON

I

Not that we are weary,
Not that we fear,
Not that we are lonely
Though never alone—
Not these, not these destroy us;
But that each rush and crash
Of mortar and shell,
Each cruel bitter shriek of bullet
That tears the wind like a blade,
Each wound on the breast of earth,
Of Demeter,* our Mother,
Wound us also,
Sever and rend the fine fabric
Of the wings of our frail souls,
Scatter into dust the bright wings
Of Psyche†

II

Impotent,
How impotent is all this clamour,
This destruction and contest. . . .
Night after night comes the moon
Haughty and perfect;
Night after night the Pleiades sing
And Orion swings his belt across the sky.
Night after night the frost
Crumbles the hard earth.

* Goddess of earth.   † The Soul.

Soon the spring will drop flowers
And patient creeping stalk and leaf
Along these barren lines
Where the huge rats scuttle
And the hawk shrieks to the carrion crow.

Can you stay them with your noise?
Then kill winter with your cannon,
Hold back Orion with your bayonets
And crush the spring leaf with your armies!

Soliloquy I

RICHARD ALDINGTON

No, I'm not afraid of death
(Not very much afraid, that is)
Either for others or myself;
Can watch them coming from the line
On the wheeled silent stretchers
And not shrink,
But munch my sandwich stoically
And make a joke when 'it' has passed.

But—the way they wobble!—
God! that makes one sick.
Dead men should be so still, austere,
And beautiful,
Not wobbling carrion roped upon a cart. . .

Well, thank God for rum.

Soliloquy II

RICHARD ALDINGTON

I was wrong, quite wrong;
The dead men are not always carrion.
After the advance,
As we went through the shattered trenches
Which the enemy had left,
We found, lying upon the fire-step,
A dead English soldier,
His head bloodily bandaged
And his closed left hand touching the earth,

More beautiful than one can tell,
More subtly coloured than a perfect Goya,
And more austere and lovely in repose
Than Angelo's hand could ever carve in stone.

Good-bye, Old Man

MACKENZIE BELL

Good-bye, old man, I seem to see
The meadow where, how happily,
You grazed, at first, a happy foal
Harmless in happiness. The whole
Green country-side had scarce another
Creature more joyous—gladsome brother
To streams, and winds and soaring-birds.

Then, later, would that halting words
Of mine, could paint my Nellie's ride

With laughing eyes, and legs astride,
Her first ride on your friendly back.
E'en now I see yon woodland track,
Soft with the fallen russet leaves.
Alack! alack! my poor heart grieves
To quit you, tortured. By what right
Are you made victim in a fight
It is not yours to comprehend?
Yea; men are hard; some day, good friend
May we judge differently; and think,
May we judge differently; and shrink
From torture given without appeal.
For me, I know not, yet can feel.

Goodbye, old man, may Death come soon
For you, I crave that only boon—
And, yet another would I seek;
May no dog scent afar your sleek
And well-kept flesh before you die;
And with his hot and famished breath,
Pollute you in the pangs of death.

Nox Mortis*

PAUL BEWSHER

The afternoon
   Flutters and dies:
The fairy moon
   Burns in the skies

* Night of Death.

As they grow darker, and the first stars shine
On Night's rich mantle—purple like warm wine.

On each white road
    Begins to crawl
The heavy toad:
    The night-birds call,
And round the trees the swift bats flit and wheel,
While from the barns the rats begin to steal.

So now must I,
    Bird of the night,
Towards the sky
    Make wheeling flight,
And bear my poison o'er the gloomy land,
And let it loose with hard unsparing hand.

The chafers boom
    With whirring wings,
And haunt the gloom
    Which twilight brings—
So in nocturnal travel do I wail
As through the night the wingèd engines sail.

Death, Grief, and Pain
    Are what I give.
O that the slain
    Might live—might live!
I know them not, for I have blindly killed,
And nameless hearts with nameless sorrow filled.

Thrice cursed War
    Which bids that I

Such death should pour
Down from the sky.
O, Star of Peace, rise swiftly in the East
That from such slaying men may be released.

For the Fallen

LAURENCE BINYON

With proud thanksgiving, a mother for her children,
England mourns for her dead across the sea.
Flesh of her flesh, they were, spirit of her spirit,
Fallen in the cause of the free.

Solemn the drums thrill; Death august and royal
Sings sorrow up into immortal spheres,
There is music in the midst of desolation
And a glory that shines upon our tears.

They went with songs to the battle, they were young,
Straight of limb, true of eye, steady and aglow.
They were staunch to the end against odds uncounted:
They fell with their faces to the foe.

They shall not grow old, as we that are left grow old:
Age shall not weary them, nor the years condemn.
At the going down of the sun and in the morning
We will remember them.

They mingle not with their laughing comrades again;
They sit no more at familiar tables of home;
They have no lot in our labour of the day-time;
They sleep beyond England's foam.

But where our desires are and our hopes profound,
Felt as a well-spring that is hidden from sight,
To the innermost heart of their own land they are
    known
As the stars are known to the Night;

As the stars that shall be bright when they are dust,
Moving in marches upon the heavenly plain;
As the stars that are starry in the time of our darkness,
To the end, to the end, they remain.

Report on Experience

EDMUND BLUNDEN

I have been young, and now am not too old;
And I have seen the righteous forsaken,
His health, his honour and his quality taken.
    This is not what we were formerly told.

I have seen a green country, useful to the race,
Knocked silly with guns and mines, its villages
    vanished,
Even the last rat and last kestrel banished—
    God bless us all, this was peculiar grace.

I knew Seraphina; nature gave her hue,
Glance, sympathy, note, like one from Eden.
I saw her smile warp, heard her lyric deaden;
    She turned to harlotry;—this I took to be new.

Say what you will, our God sees how they run.
These disillusions are His curious proving
That he loves humanity and will go on loving;
    Over there are faith, life, virtue in the sun.

War Autobiography

Written in Illness

EDMUND BLUNDEN

Heaven is clouded, mists of rain
Stream with idle motion by;
Like a tide the trees' refrain
Wearies me where pale I lie,
Thinking of sunny times that were
Even in shattered Festubert;
Stubborn joys that blossomed on
When the small golden god was gone

Who tiptoe on his spire surveyed
Yser north from Ypres creeping,
And, how many a sunset! made
A longed-for glory amid the weeping.
In how many a valley of death
Some trifling thing has given me breath,
And when the bat-like wings brushed by
What steady stars shone in the sky!

War might make his worst grimace
And still my mind in armour good
Turned aside in every place
And saw bright day through the black wood:
There the lyddite vapoured foul,
But there I got myself a rose;
By the shrapnelled lock I'd prowl
To see below the proud pike doze.

Like the first light ever streamed
New and lively past all telling,
What I dreamed of joy I dreamed,

The more opprest the more rebelling;
Trees ne'er shone so lusty green
As those in Hamel valley, eyes
Did never such right friendship mean
As his who loved my enterprise.

Thus the child was born again
In the youth, the toga's care
Flung aside—desired, found vain,
And sharp as ichor* grew the air:
But the hours passed and evermore
Harsher screamed the condor war,
The last green tree was scourged to nothing,
The stream's decay left senses loathing,

The eyes that had been strength so long
Gone, or blind, or lapt in clay,
And war grown twenty times as strong
As when I held him first at bay;
Then down and down I sunk from joy
To shrivelled age, though scarce a boy,
And knew for all my fear to die
That I with those lost friends should lie.

Now in slow imprisoned pain
Lie I in the garret bed
With this crampt and weighted brain
That scarce has power to wish me fled
To burst the vault and soar away
Into the apocalypse of day,
And so regain that tingling light
That twice has passed before my sight.

* discharge from wound.

Zero

EDMUND BLUNDEN

O rosy red, O torrent splendour
   Staining all the Orient gloom,
O celestial work of wonder—
   A million mornings in one bloom!

What, does the artist of creation
   Try some new plethora of flame,
For his eye's fresh fascination?
   Has the old cosmic fire grown tame?

In what subnatural strange awaking
   Is this body, which seems mine?
These feet towards that blood-burst making
   These ears which thunder, these hands
      which twine

On grotesque iron? Icy-clear
   The air of a mortal day shocks sense,
My shaking men pant after me here.
   The acid vapours hovering dense,

The fury whizzing in dozens dawn,
   The clattering rafters, clods calcined,
The blood in the flints and the trackway brown—
   I see I am clothed and in my right mind;

The dawn but hangs behind the goal,
   What is that artist's joy to me?
Here limps poor Jock with a gash in the poll,
   His red blood now is the red I see,

The swooning white of him, and that red!
　　These bombs in boxes, the crunch of shells,
　The second-hand flitting round; ahead!
　　It's plain we were born for this, naught else.

1914

RUPERT BROOKE

I Peace

Now, God be thanked Who has matched us with His
　　hour,
　　And caught our youth, and wakened us from sleep-
　　　ing,
With hand made sure, clear eye, and sharpened power,
　　To turn, as swimmers into cleanness leaping,
Glad from a world grown old and cold and weary,
　　Leave the sick hearts that honour could not move,
And half-men, and their dirty songs and dreary,
　　And all the little emptiness of love!

Oh! we, who have known shame, we have found release
　　there,
　　Where there's no ill, no grief, but sleep has mending,
　　Naught broken save this body, lost but breath;
Nothing to shake the laughing heart's long peace there
　　But only agony, and that has ending;
　　And the worst friend and enemy is but Death.

II Safety

Dear! of all happy in the hour, most blest
  He who has found our hid security,
Assured in the dark tides of the world that rest,
  And heard our word, 'Who is so safe as we?'
We have found safety with all things undying,
  The winds, and morning, tears of men and mirth,
The deep night, and birds singing, and clouds flying,
  And sleep, and freedom, and the autumnal earth.

We have built a house that is not for Time's throwing.
  We have gained a peace unshaken by pain for ever.
War knows no power. Safe shall be my going,
  Secretly armed against all death's endeavour;
Safe through all safety's lost; safe where men fall;
And if these poor limbs die, safest of all.

III The Dead

Blow out, you bugles, over the rich Dead!
  There's none of these so lonely and poor of old,
  But, dying, has made us rarer gifts than gold.
These laid the world away; poured out the red
Sweet wine of youth; gave up the years to be
  Of work and joy, and that unhoped serene,
  That men call age; and those who would have been,
Their sons, they gave, their immortality.

Blow, bugles, blow! They brought us, for our dearth,
  Holiness, lacked so long, and Love, and Pain.
Honour has come back, as a king, to earth,
  And paid his subjects with a royal wage;

And Nobleness walks in our ways again;
    And we have come into our heritage.

IV The Dead

These hearts were woven of human joys and cares,
    Washed marvellously with sorrow, swift to mirth.
The years had given them kindness. Dawn was theirs,
    And sunset, and the colours of the earth.
These had seen movement, and heard music; known
    Slumber and waking; loved; gone proudly friended;
Felt the quick stir of wonder; sat alone;
    Touched flowers and furs and cheeks. All this is
        ended.

There are waters blown by changing winds to laughter
And lit by the rich skies, all day. And after,
    Frost, with a gesture, stays the waves that dance
And wandering loveliness. He leaves a white
    Unbroken glory, a gathered radiance,
A width, a shining peace, under the night.

V The Soldier

If I should die, think only this of me:
    That there's some corner of a foreign field
That is for ever England. There shall be
    In that rich earth a richer dust concealed;
A dust whom England bore, shaped, made aware,
    Gave, once, her flowers to love, her ways to roam,
A body of England's, breathing English air,
    Washed by the rivers, blest by suns of home.

55

And think this heart, all evil shed away,
    A pulse in the eternal mind, no less
        Gives somewhere back the thoughts by England
            given;
Her sights and sounds; dreams happy as her day;
    And laughter, learnt of friends; and gentleness,
        In hearts at peace, under an English heaven.

From the Somme

LESLIE COULSON

In other days I sang of simple things,
    Of summer dawn, and summer noon and night,
The dewy grass, the dew-wet fairy rings,
    The larks' long golden flight.

Deep in the forest I made melody
    While squirrels cracked their hazel nuts on high,
Or I would cross the wet sand to the sea
    And sing to sea and sky.

When came the silvered silence of the night
    I stole to casements over scented lawns,
And softly sang of love and love's delight
    To mute white marble fauns.

Oft in the tavern parlour I would sing
    Of morning sun upon the mountain vine,
And, calling for a chorus, sweep the string
    In praise of good red wine.

I played with all the toys the gods provide,
    I sang my songs and made glad holiday.
Now I have cast my broken toys aside
    And flung my lute away.

A singer once, I now am fain to weep.
    Within my soul I feel strange music swell,
Vast chants of tragedy too deep—too deep
    For my poor lips to tell.

On the Wings of the Morning

JEFFERY DAY

A sudden roar, a mighty rushing sound,
    a jolt or two, a smoothly sliding rise,
a tumbled blur of disappearing ground,
    and then all sense of motion slowly dies.
        Quiet and calm, and earth slips past below,
        as underneath a bridge still waters flow.

My turning wing inclines towards the ground;
    The ground itself glides up with graceful swing
and at the plane's far tip twirls slowly round,
    then drops from sight again beneath the wing
        to slip away serenely as before,
        a cubist-patterned carpet on the floor.

Hills gently sink and valleys gently fill.
    The flattened fields grow ludicrously small;
slowly they pass beneath and slower still
    until they hardly seem to move at all.
        Then suddenly they disappear from sight,
        hidden by fleeting wisps of faded white.

The wing-tips, faint and dripping, dimly show,
    blurred by the wreaths of mist that intervene.
Weird, half-seen shadows flicker to and fro
    across the pallid fog-bank's blinding screen.
        At last the choking mists release their hold,
        and all the world is silver, blue, and gold.

The air is clear, more clear than sparkling wine;
    compared with this, wine is a turgid brew.
The far horizon makes a clean-cut line
    between the silver and the depthless blue.
        Out of the snow-white level reared on high
        glittering hills surge up to meet the sky.

Outside the wind screen's shelter gales may race:
    but in the seat a cool and gentle breeze
blows steadily upon my grateful face.
    As I sit motionless and at my ease,
        contented just to loiter in the sun
        and gaze around me till the day is done.

And so I sit, half sleeping, half awake,
    dreaming a happy dream of golden days,
until at last, with a reluctant shake
    I rouse myself, and with a lingering gaze
        at all the splendour of the shining plain
        make ready to come down to earth again.

The engine stops: a pleasant silence reigns—
    silence, not broken, but intensified
by the soft, sleepy wires' insistent strains,
    that rise and fall, as with a sweeping glide
        I slither down the well-oiled sides of space,
        towards a lower, less enchanted place.

The clouds draw nearer, changing as they come.
Now, like a flash, fog grips me by the throat.
Down goes the nose: at once the wires' low hum
   begins to rise in volume and in note,
      till, as I hurtle from the choking cloud
      it swells into a scream, high-pitched, and loud.

The scattered hues and shades of green and brown
   fashion themselves into the land I know,
turning and twisting, as I spiral down
   towards the landing-ground; till, skimming low,
      I glide with slackening speed across the ground,
      and come to rest with lightly grating sound.

Five Souls

W. N. EWER

FIRST SOUL

I was a peasant of the Polish plain;
I left my plough because the message ran:—
Russia in danger, needed every man
To save her from the Teuton; and was slain.
*I gave my life for freedom—This I know
For those who bade me fight had told me so.*

SECOND SOUL

I was a Tyrolese, a mountaineer;
I gladly left my mountain home to fight
Against the brutal treacherous Muscovite;
And died in Poland on a Cossack spear.
*I gave my life for freedom—This I know
For those who bade me fight had told me so.*

THIRD SOUL

I worked in Lyons at my weaver's loom,
When suddenly the Prussian despot hurled
His felon blow at France and at the world;
Then I went forth to Belgium and my doom.
I gave my life for freedom—This I know
For those who bade me fight had told me so.

FOURTH SOUL

I owned a vineyard by the wooded Main,
Until the Fatherland begirt by foes
Lusting her downfall, called me, and I rose
Swift to the call—and died in far Lorraine.
I gave my life for freedom—This I know
For those who bade me fight had told me so.

FIFTH SOUL

I worked in a great shipyard by the Clyde;
There came a sudden word of wars declared,
Of Belgium, peaceful, helpless, unprepared,
Asking our aid: I joined the ranks, and died.
I gave my life for freedom—This I know
For those who bade me fight had told me so.

What the Orderly Dog Saw

A Winter Landscape

FORD MADOX FORD

I

The seven white peacocks against the castle wall
In the high trees and the dusk are like tapestry,
The sky being orange, the high wall a purple barrier

The canal, dead silver in the dusk
    And you are far away.
Yet I can see indefinite miles of mountains.
Little lights shining in rows in the dark of them;
Infinite miles of marshes.
Thin wisps of mist, shimmering like blue webs
Over the dusk of them, great curves and horns
    of sea
And dusk and dusk and the little village
    And you, sitting in the firelight.

II

Around me are the two hundred and forty men of
    B Company
Mud-coloured.
Going about their avocations,
Resting between their practice of the art
Of killing men.
As I too rest between my practice
Of the Art of killing men.
Their pipes glow above the mud and their mud
    colour, moving like fireflies beneath the trees,
I too being mud-coloured
Beneath the trees and the peacocks.
When they come up to me in the dusk
They start, stiffen and salute, almost invisibly.
And the forty-two prisoners from the Battalion
    guardroom
Crouch over the tea cans in the shadow of the wall.
And the bread hunks glimmer, beneath the peacocks,
And you are far away.

III

Presently I shall go in,
I shall write down the names of the forty-two

Prisoners in the Battalion guardroom
On fair white foolscap.
Their names, rank, and regimental numbers,
Corps, Companies, Punishments and Offences,
Remarks, and By whom Confined.
Yet in spite of all I shall see only
The infinite miles of dark mountain,
The infinite miles of dark marshland,
Great curves and horns of sea
The little village.
And you,
Sitting in the firelight.

Cardiff Castle, 12 | 12 | 15

Ammunition Column

GILBERT FRANKAU

I am only a cog in a giant machine, a link of an endless chain:
*And the rounds are drawn, and the rounds are fired, and the empties
    return again;*
Railroad, lorry, and limber; battery, column, and park;
*To the shelf where the set fuse waits the breech, from the quay where the
    shells embark.*
We have watered and fed, and eaten our beef; the long dull day
    drags by.
As I sit here watching our 'Archibalds' *strafing** an empty sky;
Puff and flash on the far-off blue round the speck one guesses
    the plane—
Smoke and spark of the gun-machine that is fed by the endless
    chain.

* pounding.

I am only a cog in a giant machine, a little link in the chain,
Waiting a word from the wagon-lines that the guns are hungry
again:
Column-wagon to battery-wagon, and battery-wagon to gun;
To the loader kneeling 'twixt trail and wheel from the shops where the
steam-lathes run.
There's a lone-mule braying against the line where the mud
cakes fetlock-deep!
There's a lone soul humming a hint of a song in the barn where
the drivers sleep;
And I hear the push of the orderly's horse as he canters him
down the lane—
Another cog in the gun-machine, a link in the selfsame chain.

I am only a cog in a giant machine, but a vital link in the chain;
And the Captain has sent from the wagon-line to fill his wagons
again;—
From wagon-limber to gunpit dump; from loader's forearm at breech,
To the working party that melts away when the shrapnel bullets screech.—
So the restless section pulls out once in column of route from
the right,
At the tail of a blood-red afternoon; so the flux of another
night
Bears back the wagons we fill at dawn to the sleeping column
again . . .
Cog on cog in the gun-machine, link on link in the chain!

Happy is England Now

JOHN FREEMAN

There is not anything more wonderful
Than a great people moving towards the deep
Of an unguessed and unfeared future; nor

Is aught so dear of all held dear before
As the new passion stirring in their veins
When the destroying dragon wakes from sleep.

Happy is England now, as never yet!
And though the sorrows of the slow days fret
Her faithfullest children, grief itself is proud.
Ev'n the warm beauty of this spring and summer
That turns to bitterness turns then to gladness
Since for this England the beloved ones died.

Happy is England in the brave that die
For wrongs not hers and wrongs so sternly hers;
Happy in those that give, give, and endure
The pain that never the new years may cure;
Happy in all her dark woods, green fields, towns,
Her hills and rivers and her chafing seas.

Whate'er was dear before is dearer now.
There's not a bird singing upon this bough
But sings the sweeter in our English ears:
There's not a nobleness of heart, hand, brain,
But shines the purer; happiest is England now
In those that fight, and watch with pride and tears.

To E. T.*

ROBERT FROST

I slumbered with your poems on my breast
Spread open as I dropped them half-read through
Like dove wings on a figure on a tomb
To see, if in a dream they brought of you.

* Edward Thomas.

64

I might not have the chance I missed in life
Through some delay, and call you to your face
First soldier, and then poet, and then both,
Who died a soldier-poet of your race.

I meant, you meant, that nothing should remain
Unsaid between us, brother, and this remained—
And one thing more that was not then to say:
The Victory for what it lost and gained.

You went to meet the shell's embrace of fire
On Vimy Ridge; and when you fell that day
The war seemed over more for you than me,
But now for me than you—the other way.

How over, though, for even me who knew
The foe thrust back unsafe beyond the Rhine,
If I was not to speak of it to you
And see you pleased once more with words of
     mine?

Mad

WILFRID GIBSON

Neck-deep in mud,
He mowed and raved—
He who had braved
The field of blood—
And as a lad
Just out of school
Yelled—*April fool!*
And laughed like mad.

In The Ambulance

WILFRID GIBSON

Two rows of cabbages,
Two of curly-greens,
Two rows of early peas,
Two of kidney-beans.

That's what he keeps muttering,
Making such a song,
Keeping other chaps awake
The whole night long.

Both his legs are shot away,
And his head is light,
So he keeps on muttering
All the blessed night:

Two rows of cabbages,
Two of curly-greens,
Two rows of early peas,
Two of kidney beans.

The Bayonet

WILFRID GIBSON

This bloody steel
Has killed a man.
I heard him squeal
As on I ran.

He watched me come
With wagging head.

I pressed it home,
And he was dead.

Though clean and clear
I've wiped the steel,
I still can hear
That dying squeal.

Country at War

ROBERT GRAVES

And what of home—how goes it, boys,
While we die here in stench and noise?
'The hill stands up and hedges wind
Over the crest and drop behind;
Here swallows dip and wild things go
On peaceful errands to and fro
Across the sloping meadow floor,
And make no guess at blasting war.
In woods that fledge the round hill-shoulder
Leaves shoot and open, fall and moulder,
And shoot again. Meadows yet show
Alternate white of drifted snow
And daisies. Children play at shop,
Warm days, on the flat boulder-top,
With wildflower coinage, and the wares
Are bits of glass and unripe pears.
Crows perch upon the backs of sheep,
The wheat goes yellow: women reap,
Autumn winds ruffle brook and pond,
Flutter the hedge and fly beyond.
So the first things of nature run,
And stand not still for any one,

Contemptuous of the distant cry
Wherewith you harrow earth and sky.
And high French clouds, praying to be
Back, back in peace beyond the sea,
Where nature with accustomed round
Sweeps and garnishes the ground
With kindly beauty, warm or cold—
Alternate seasons never old:
Heathen, how furiously you rage,
Cursing this blood and brimstone age,
How furiously against your will
You kill and kill again, and kill:
All thought of peace behind you cast,
Till like small boys with fear aghast,
Each cries for God to understand,
"I could not help it, it was my hand".'

The Leveller

ROBERT GRAVES

Near Martinpuisch that night of hell
Two men were struck by the same shell,
Together tumbling in one heap
Senseless and limp like slaughtered sheep.

One was a pale eighteen-year-old,
Girlish and thin and not too bold,
Pressed for the war ten years too soon,
The shame and pity of his platoon.

The other came from far-off lands
With bristling chin and whiskered hands,
He had known death and hell before
In Mexico and Ecuador.

Yet in his death this cut-throat wild
Groaned 'Mother! Mother!' like a child,
While that poor innocent in man's clothes
Died cursing God with brutal oaths.

Old Sergeant Smith, kindest of men,
Wrote out two copies there and then
Of his accustomed funeral speech
To cheer the womenfolk of each.

He died a hero's death and we
His comrades of 'A' Company
Send heartfelt sympathies, we shall
All greatly miss so true a pal.

Into Battle

JULIAN GRENFELL

The naked earth is warm with spring,
  And with green grass and bursting trees
Leans to the sun's gaze glorying,
  And quivers in the sunny breeze;
And life is colour and warmth and light,
  And a striving evermore for these;
And he is dead who will not fight;
  And who dies fighting has increase.

The fighting man shall from the sun
  Take warmth, and life from the glowing earth;
Speed with the light-foot winds to run,
  And with the trees to newer birth;
And find, when fighting shall be done,
  Great rest, and fullness after dearth.

All the bright company of Heaven
    Hold him in their high comradeship,
The Dog-Star, and the Sisters Seven,
    Orion's Belt and sworded hip.

The woodland trees that stand together,
    They stand to him each one a friend;
They gently speak in the windy weather;
    They guide to valley and ridge's end.

The kestrel hovering by day,
    And the little owls that call by night,
Bid him be swift and keen as they,
    As keen of ear, as swift of sight.

The blackbird sings to him, 'Brother, brother,
    If this be the last song you shall sing,
Sing well, for you may not sing another;
    Brother, sing.'

In dreary, doubtful, waiting hours,
    Before the brazen frenzy starts,
The horses show him nobler powers;
    O patient eyes, courageous hearts!

And when the burning moment breaks,
    And all things else are out of mind,
And only joy of battle takes
    Him by the throat, and makes him blind,

Through joy and blindness he shall know,
    Not caring much to know, that still
Nor lead nor steel shall reach him, so
    That it be not the Destined Will.

The thundering line of battle stands,
  And in the air death moans and sings;
But Day shall clasp him with strong hands,
  And Night shall fold him in soft wings.

Servitude

IVOR GURNEY

If it were not for England, who would bear
This heavy servitude one moment more?
To keep a brothel, sweep and wash the floor
Of filthiest hovels were noble to compare
With this brass-cleaning life. Now here, now there
Harried in foolishness, scanned curiously o'er
By fools made brazen by conceit, and store
Of antique witticisms thin and bare.

Only the love of comrades sweetens all,
Whose laughing spirit will not be outdone.
As night-watching men wait for the sun
To hearten them, so wait I on such boys
As neither brass nor Hell-fire may appal,
Nor guns, nor sergeant-major's bluster and noise.

The Target

IVOR GURNEY

I shot him, and it had to be
One of us! 'Twas him or me.
'Couldn't be helped,' and none can blame
Me, for you would do the same.

My mother, she can't sleep for fear
Of what might be a-happening here
To me. Perhaps it might be best
To die, and set her fears at rest.

For worst is worst, and worry's done.
Perhaps he was the only son . . .
Yet God keeps still, and does not say
A word of guidance any way.

Well, if they get me, first I'll find
That boy, and tell him all my mind,
And see who felt the bullet worst,
And ask his pardon, if I durst.

All's a tangle, Here's my job.
A man might rave, or shout, or sob;
And God He takes no sort of heed.
This is a bloody mess indeed.

Before Marching, And After

In Memoriam F.W.G.

THOMAS HARDY

Orion swung southward aslant
Where the starved Egdon pine-trees had thinned,
The Pleiads aloft seemed to pant
With the heather that twitched in the wind;
But he looked on indifferent to sights such as these,
Unswayed by love, friendship, home joy or home sorrow,
And wondered to what he would march on the morrow.

The crazed household clock with its whirr
Rang midnight within as he stood,
He heard the low sighing of her
Who had striven from his birth for his good;
But he still only asked the spring starlight, the breeze,
What great thing or small thing his history would borrow
From that Game with Death he would play on the morrow.

When the heath wore the robe of late summer,
And the fuchsia-bells, hot in the sun,
Hung red by the door, a quick comer
Brought tidings that marching was done
For him who had joined in that game overseas
Where Death stood to win; though his memory would
    borrow
A brightness therefrom not to die on the morrow.

'And there was a Great Calm'

On the signing of the Armistice, November 11th, 1918

THOMAS HARDY

I

There had been years of Passion—scorching, cold,
And much Despair, and Anger heaving high,
Care whitely watching, Sorrows manifold,
Among the young, among the weak and old,
And the pensive Spirit of Pity whispered, 'Why?'

II

Men had not paused to answer. Foes distraught
Pierced the thinned peoples in a brute-like blindness,
Philosophies that sages long had taught,

And Selflessness, were as an unknown thought,
And 'Hell!' and 'Shell!' were yapped at Loving-
    kindness.

III

The feeble folk at home had grown full-used
To 'dug-outs,' 'snipers,' 'Huns,' from the war-adept
In the mornings heard, and at evetides perused;
To day-dreamt men in millions, when they mused—
To nightmare-men in millions when they slept.

IV

Waking to wish existence timeless, null,
Sirius they watched above where armies fell;
He seemed to check his flapping when, in the lull
Of night a boom came thencewise, like the dull
Plunge of a stone dropped into some deep well.

V

So when old hopes that earth was bettering slowly
Were dead and damned, there sounded 'War is done!'
One morrow. Said the bereft, and meek, and lowly,
'Will men some day be given to grace? yea, wholly,
And in good sooth, as our dreams used to run?'

VI

Breathless they paused. Out there men raised their
    glance,
To where had stood those poplars lank and lopped,
As they had raised it through the four years' dance
Of Death in the now familiar flats of France;
And murmured, 'Strange, this! How? All firing
    stopped?'

74

VII

Aye; all was hushed. The about-to-fire fired not,
The aimed-at moved away in trance-lipped song.
One checkless regiment slung a clinching shot
And turned. The Spirit of Irony smirked out, 'What?
Spoil peradventures woven of Rage and Wrong?'

VIII

Thenceforth no flying fires inflamed the gray,
No hurtlings shook the dewdrop from the thorn,
No moan perplexed the mute bird on the spray;
Worn horses mused: 'We are not whipped today';
No left-winged engines blurred the moon's thin
    horn.

IX

Calm fell. From heaven distilled a clemency;
There was peace on earth, and silence in the sky;
Some could, some could not, shake off misery:
The Sinister Spirit sneered: 'It had to be!'
And again the Spirit of Pity whispered, 'Why?'

Autumn in Prison

F. W. HARVEY

Here where no tree changes,
    Here in a prison of pine,
I think how Autumn ranges
    The country that is mine.

There—rust upon the chill breeze—
    The woodland leaf now whirls;

There sway the yellowing birches
  Like dainty dancing girls.

Oh, how the leaves are dancing
  With Death at Lassington!
And Death is now enhancing
  Beauty I walked upon.

The roads with leaves are littered,
  Yellow, brown and red;
The homes where robins twittered
  Lie ruin; but instead

Gaunt arms of stretching giants
  Stand in the azure air,
Cutting the sky in pattern
  So common, yet so fair,

The heart is kindled by it,
  And lifted as with wine,
In Lassington and Highnam—
  The woodlands that were mine.

If we return

(Rondeau)

F. W. HARVEY

If we return, will England be
Just England still to you and me—
The place where we must earn our bread?
We, who have walked among the dead,
And watched the smile of agony,

And seen the price of Liberty,
Which we have taken carelessly
From other hands. Nay, we shall dread:
    If we return.

Dread lest we hold blood-guiltily
The things that men have died to free.
Oh, English fields shall blossom red
For all the blood that has been shed,
By men whose guardians are we,
    If we return.

Back to Rest

Composed while marching to Rest Camp after severe fighting at Loos

WILLIAM NOEL HODGSON

A leaping wind from England,
    The skies without a stain,
Clean cut against the morning
    Slim poplars after rain,
The foolish noise of sparrows
    And starlings in a wood—
After the grime of battle
    We know that these are good.

Death whining down from Heaven,
    Death roaring from the ground,
Death stinking in every nostril,
    Death shrill in every sound,
Doubting, we charged and conquered—
    Hopeless we struck and stood.
Now when the fight is ended
    We know that it was good.

We that have seen the strongest
　　Cry like a beaten child,
The sanest eye unholy,
　　The cleanest hands defiled,
We that have known the heart blood
　　Less then the lees of wine,
We that have seen men broken,
　　We know man is divine.

Before Action*

WILLIAM NOEL HODGSON

By all the glories of the day
　　And the cool evening's benison,
By that last sunset touch that lay
　　Upon the hills when day was done,
By beauty lavishly outpoured
　　And blessings carelessly received,
By all the days that I have lived
　　Make me a soldier, Lord.

By all of man's hopes and fears,
　　And all the wonders poets sing,
The laughter of unclouded years,
　　And every sad and lovely thing;
By the romantic ages stored
　　With high endeavour that was his,
By all his mad catastrophes
　　Make me a man, O Lord.

I, that on my familiar hill
　　Saw with uncomprehending eyes

* written two days before his death on 1 July 1916.

A hundred of Thy sunsets spill
  Their fresh and sanguine sacrifice,
Ere the sun swings his noonday sword
  Must say goodbye to all of this;—
By all delights that I shall miss,
  Help me to die, O Lord.

Armageddon—and After

LAURENCE HOUSMAN

We fought at Armageddon for the freedom of the world:
  I fought and you fought, and here our bones lie mixed.
By the master-hands which held us, eastward and westward
    hurled,
We were shattered, we fell down, for the place and time
    were fixed.

Tell me, O brother Bone, what here remains to know:
  Marched we as comrades then, or foemen, ere we died?
Was it my hand or yours which dealt the blinding blow:
  Was it your hand or mine which turned the blow aside?

Took I my brother's life: what better life was mine?
  Fought I for freedom—of freedom so bereft?
Had I the clearer sight to read the Heavenly sign?
  Had I the cleaner heart, to keep my hands from theft?

We fought at Armageddon for the freedom of mankind.
  And while we fought, behind us freedom was bought and
    sold!
The light that lit these sockets is out, and we are blind.
  Now with blind eyes we read; now with dead hands can
    hold.

Bone to my bone you lie, companion of my pains!
    What link of life is this, which binds us wrist to wrist?
These, brother, these are not links but only chains.
    Worn by the living, that dying lips have kissed.

Millions we marched; and the rattle of the drums
    Drowned the rattle of our chains, and the shouting held
        our ranks.
For sweet to our ears was 'The conquering hero comes,'
    And sweet to our hearts 'A grateful Country's thanks.'

We fought at Armageddon for the brotherhood of Man;
    And safe within their fences the tricksters plied their trade.
'Twas the old fight we fought; and it ends as it began:
    The gamblers held their hands till the Last Trump was
        played.

We fought at Armageddon for the freedom of mankind:
    I fought, and you fought, and here our bones lie strewn.
The flesh is stript from off us, the chains remain behind,
    And the freedom that we fought for is an unremembered
        tune.

An Oxford Retrospect: May 1915

DYNELEY HUSSEY

May!—and I am no more among your spires,
    Dear Mother-city of my soul.
May!—and my heart hath new desires,
    My spirit seeks another goal.

The lilac purples in the meadows green,
The avenues of elms I walked between

Cast over Christ Church walk their welcome shade.
Now in the College garden tulips tall
Nod to the gnarled wisteria on the wall,
    And bright laburnum clusters gild the glade.

Now livid snakesheads bloom in Iffley mead,
And golden king-cups and pale cuckoo-weed,
    That children gather against market-day.
O'er the cloud-dappled Cumnor hills the shade
Chases the sunlight—there I oft have strayed
    And watched dun milch-cows munch the hours
    away.

The river flows as ever 'neath the trees,
But I no longer take thereon my ease
    Where a pink hawthorn overhangs the stream.
Ah! lazy, languid idlings on the Cher,
Sweet lotus-eatings, while my soul ranged far,
    In empty musing, through a vain day-dream.

Ah! days of yester-year, whose hours flew by,
As winds blow past the tent wherein I lie,
    Heedless I let you go nor knew your span.
And yet—I would not have you back again,
Even amid the misery and pain
    That now is making of the boy a man.

Next May! And if I lie in some cold grave
    Dear Mother-city of my soul,
I am content to yield the life you gave
    If but I nobly reach the goal.

Dooleysprudence

Who is the man when all the gallant nations run to war
Goes home to have his dinner by the very first cablecar
And as he eats his canteloupe* contorts himself in mirth
To read the blatant bulletins of the rulers of the earth?
    It's Mr Dooley,†
    Mr Dooley,
    The coolest chap our country ever knew
    'They are out to collar
    The dime and dollar'
    Says Mr Dooley-ooley-ooley-oo.

Who is the fully fellow who declines to go to church
Since pope and priest and parson left the poor man in the
    lurch
And taught their flocks the only way to save all human souls
Was piercing human bodies through with dumdum bullet-
    holes?
    It's Mr Dooley,
    Mr Dooley,
    The mildest man our country knew
    'Who will release us
    From Jingo Jesus'
    Prays Mr Dooley-ooley-ooley-oo.

Who is the meek philosopher who doesn't care a damn
About the yellow peril or problem of Siam
And disbelieves that British Tar is water from life's fount
And will not gulp the gospel of the German on the Mount?
    It's Mr Dooley,
    Mr Dooley,
    The broadest brain our country ever knew

* Melon.   † Embassy official in Switzerland.

'The curse of Moses
On both your houses'
Cries Mr Dooley-ooley-ooley-oo.

Who is the cheerful imbecile who lights his long chibouk*
With pages of the pandect,† penal code and Doomsday Book
And wonders why bald justices are bound by law to wear
A toga and a wig made out of someone else's hair?
    It's Mr Dooley,
    Mr Dooley,
    The finest fool our country ever knew
    'They took that toilette
    From Pontius Pilate'
    Thinks Mr Dooley-ooley-ooley-oo.

Who is the man who says he'll go the whole and perfect hog
Before he pays the income tax or licence for a dog
And when he licks a postage stamp regards with smiling
    scorn
The face of king or emperor or snout of unicorn?
    It's Mr Dooley,
    Mr Dooley,
    The wildest wag our country ever knew
    'O my poor tummy
    His backside gummy!'
    Moans Mr Dooley-ooley-ooley-oo.

Who is the tranquil gentleman who won't salute the State
Or serve Nebuchadnezzar or proletariat
But thinks that every son of man has quite enough to do
To paddle down the stream of life his personal canoe?
    It's Mr Dooley,
    Mr Dooley,

* tobacco-pipe. † code of laws.

The wisest wight our country ever knew
'Poor Europe ambles
Like sheep to shambles'
Sighs Mr Dooley-ooley-ooley-oo.

'For all we have and are'

RUDYARD KIPLING

For all we have and are,
For all our children's fate,
Stand up and take the war,
The Hun is at the gate!
Our world has passed away,
In wantonness o'erthrown.
There is nothing left to-day
But steel and fire and stone!
  Though all we knew depart,
  The old Commandments stand:—
  'In courage keep your heart,
  In strength lift up your hand.'

Once more we hear the word
That sickened earth of old:—
'No law except the Sword
Unsheathed and uncontrolled.'
Once more it knits mankind,
Once more the nations go
To meet and break and bind
A crazed and driven foe.

Comfort, content, delight,
The ages' slow-bought gain,
They shrivelled in a night.

Only ourselves remain
To face the naked days
In silent fortitude,
Through perils and dismays
Renewed and re-renewed.
   Though all we made depart,
   The old Commandments stand:—
   'In patience keep your heart,
   In strength lift up your hand.'

No easy hopes or lies
Shall bring us to our goal,
But iron sacrifice
Of body, will, and soul.
There is but one task for all—
One life for each to give.
Who stands if Freedom fall?
Who dies if England live?

from 'Epitaphs of the War 1914-1918'

RUDYARD KIPLING

Bombed in London

On land and sea I strove with anxious care
To escape conscription. It was in the air!

A Dead Statesman

I could not dig: I dared not rob:
Therefore I lied to please the mob.
Now all my lies are proved untrue
And I must face the men I slew.
What tale shall serve me here among
Mine angry and defrauded young?

A Son

My son was killed while laughing at some jest. I would I
  knew
What it was, and it might serve me in time when jests are few.

The Favour

Death favoured me from the first, well knowing I could not
  endure
  To wait on him day by day. He quitted my betters and
  came
Whistling over the fields, and, when he had made all sure,
  'Thy line is at end,' he said, 'but at least I have saved its
  name.'

Unknown Female Corpse

Headless, lacking foot and hand,
Horrible I come to land.
I beseech all women's sons
Know I was a mother once.

We Have Gone too Far

D. H. LAWRENCE

We have gone too far, oh, very much too far,
Only attend to the noiseless multitudes
Of ghosts that throng about out muffled hearts.

Only behold the ghosts, the ghosts of the slain,
Behold them homeless and houseless, without complaint
Of their patient waiting upon us, the throne of ghosts.

And say, what matters any more, what matters,
Save the cold ghosts that homeless flock about
Our serried hearts, drifting without a place?

What matters any more, but only love?
There's only love that matters any more.
There's only love, the rest is all outspent.

Let us receive our ghosts and give them place,
Open the ranks, and let them in our hearts,
And lay them deep in love, lay them to sleep.

The foe can take our goods, our homes and land,
Also the lives that still he may require,
But leave us still to love, still leave us love.

Leave us to take our ghosts into our hearts,
To lap them round with love, and lay them by
To sleep at last in immemorial love.

We let the weapons slip from out our hands,
We loose our grip, and we unstrain our eyes,
We let our souls be pure and vulnerable.

We cover the houseless dead, so they sleep in peace,
We yield the enemy his last demands,
So he too may be healed, be soothed to peace.

For now the hosts of homeless ghosts do throng
To many about us, so we wander about
Blind with the gossamer of prevalent death.

But let us free our eyes, and look beyond
This serried ecstasy of prevalent death,
And pass beyond, with the foe and the homeless ghosts.

Let us rise up and go from out this grey
Last twilight of the Gods, to find again
The lost Hesperides where love is pure.

For we have gone too far, oh much too far
Towards the darkness and the shadow of death;
Let us turn back, lest we should all be lost.

Let us go back now, though we give up all
The treasure and the vaunt we ever had,
Let us go back, the only way of love.

from 'New Heaven and Earth'

D. H. LAWRENCE

IV

At last came death, sufficiency of death,
and that at last relieved me, I died.
I buried my beloved; it was good, I buried myself and was gone.
War came, and every hand raised to murder!
very good, very good, every hand raised to murder!
Very good, very good, I am a murderer!
It is good, I can murder and murder, and see them fall,
the mutilated, horror-struck youths, a multitude
one on another, and then in clusters together
smashed, all oozing with blood, and burned in heaps
going up in a foetid* smoke to get rid of them,
the murdered bodies of youths and men in heaps
and heaps and heaps and horrible reeking heaps
till it is almost enough, till I am reduced perhaps;
Thousands and thousands of gaping, hideous foul dead
that are youths and men and me

* evil-smelling.

being burned with oil, and consumed in corrupt thick smoke,
    that rolls
and taints and blacken the sky, till at last it is dark, dark as
    night, or death, or hell
and I am dead, and trodden to nought in the smoke-sodden
    tomb;
dead and trodden to nought in the sour black earth
of the tomb; dead and trodden to nought, trodden to nought.

V

God, but it is good to have died and been trodden out,
trodden to nought in sour, dead earth,
quite to nought,
absolutely to nothing
nothing
nothing
nothing.

For when it is quite, quite nothing, then it is everything.
When I am trodden quite out, quite, quite out,
every vestige gone, then I am here
risen, accomplishing a resurrection
risen, not born again, but risen, body the same as before,
new beyond knowledge of newness, alive beyond life,
proud beyond inkling or furthest conception of pride,
living where life was never yet dreamed of, nor hinted at,
here, in the other world, still terrestrial
myself, the same as before, yet unaccountably new.

After Court Martial

FRANCIS LEDWIDGE

My mind is not my mind, therefore
I take no heed of what men say,

89

I lived ten thousand years before
God cursed the town of Nineveh.

The Present is a dream I see
Of horror and loud sufferings,
At dawn a bird will waken me
Unto my place among the kings.

And though men called me a vile name,
And all my dream companions gone,
'Tis I the soldier bears the shame,
Not I the king of Babylon.

Recruiting

E. A. MACKINTOSH

'Lads, you're wanted, go and help,'
On the railway carriage wall
Stuck the poster, and I thought
Of the hands that penned the call.

Fat civilians wishing they
'Could go and fight the Hun.'
Can't you see them thanking God
That they're over forty-one?

Girls with feathers, vulgar songs—
Washy verse on England's need—
God—and don't we damned well know
How the message ought to read.

'Lads, you're wanted! over there,'
Shiver in the morning dew,

More poor devils like yourselves
Waiting to be killed by you.

Go and help to swell the names
In the casualty lists.
Helps to make the column's stuff
For the blasted journalists.

Help to keep them nice and safe
From the wicked German foe.
Don't let him come over here!
'Lads, you're wanted—out you go.'

There's a better word than that,
Lads, and can't you hear it come
From a million men that call
You to share their martyrdom?

Leave the harlots still to sing
Comic songs about the Hun,
Leave the fat old men to say
Now *we've* got them on the run.

Better twenty honest years
Than their dull three score and ten.
Lads, you're wanted. Come and learn
To live and die with honest men.

You shall learn what men can do
If you will but pay the price,
Learn the gaiety and strength
In the gallant sacrifice.

Take your risk of life and death
Underneath the open sky.

Live clean or go out quick—
Lads, you're wanted. Come and die.

The Face

FREDERIC MANNING

Out of the smoke of men's wrath,
The red mist of anger,
Suddenly,
As a wraith of sleep,
A boy's face, white and tense,
Convulsed with terror and hate,
The lips trembling . . .

Then a red smear, falling . . .
I thrist aside the cloud, as it were tangible,
Blinded with a mist of blood,
The face cometh again
As a wraith of sleep:
A boy's face delicate and blonde,
The very mask of God,
Broken.

A Shell

FREDERIC MANNING

Here we are all, naked as Greeks,
Killing the lice in our shirts:
Suddenly the air is torn asunder,
Ripped as coarse silk,
Then a dull thud . . .
We are all squatting.

'Lord, I owe Thee a Death'

(*Richard Hooker*)

ALICE MEYNELL

Man pays that debt with new munificence,
    Not piecemeal now, not slowly, by the old:
Not grudgingly, by the effaced thin pence,
    But greatly and in gold.

Youth in Arms: IV

Carrion

HAROLD MONRO

It is plain now what you are. Your head has dropped
Into a furrow. And the lovely curve
Of your strong leg has wasted and is propped
Against a ridge of the ploughed land's watery swerve.

You are swayed on waves of the silent ground;
You clutch and claim with passionate grasp of your
    fingers
The dip of earth in which your body lingers;
If you are not found,
In a little while your limbs will fall apart;
The birds will take some, but the earth will take most
    your heart.

You are fuel for a coming spring if they leave you here;
The crop that will rise from your bones is healthy bread.
You died—we know you—without a word of fear,
And as they loved you living I love you dead.

No girl would kiss you. But then
No girls would ever kiss the earth
In the manner they hug the lips of men:
You are not known to them in this, your second birth.

No coffin-cover will now cram
Your body in a shell of lead;
Earth will not fall on you from the spade with a slam,
But will fold and enclose you slowly, you living dead.

Hush, I hear the guns. Are you still asleep?
Surely I saw you a little heave to reply.
I can hardly think you will not turn over and creep
Along the furrows trenchward as if to die.

Boy

ROBERT NICHOLS

In a far field, away from England, lies
A Boy I friended with a care like love;
All day the wide earth aches, the cold wind cries,
The melancholy clouds drive on above.

There, separate from him by a little span,
Two eagle cousins, generous, reckless, free,
Two Grenfells,* lie, and my Boy is made man,
One with these elder knights of chivalry.

Boy, who expected not this dreadful day,
Yet leaped, a soldier, at the sudden call,
Drank as your fathers, deeper though than they,
The soldier's cup of anguish, blood, and gall,

* Julian and William Grenfell, the poet and his cousin.

Not now as friend, but as a soldier, I
Salute you fallen; for the Soldier's name
Our greatest honour is, if worthily
These wayward hearts assume and bear the same:

The Soldier's is a name none recognize,
Saving his fellows. Deeds are all his flowers.
He lives, he toils, he suffers, and he dies,
And if not all in vain this is his dower:

The Soldier is the Martyr of a nation,
Expresses but is subject to its will;
His is the Pride ennobles Resignation,
As his the rebel Spirit-to-fulfil.

Anonymous, he takes his country's name,
Becomes its blindest vassal—though its lord
By force of arms; its shame is called his shame,
As its the glory gathered by his sword.

Lonely he is: he has nor friend nor lover,
Sith in his body he is dedicate. . . .
His comrades only share his life, or offer
Their further deeds to one more heart oblate.

Living, he's made an 'Argument Beyond'
For others' peace; but when hot wars have birth,
For all his brothers' safety becomes bond
To Fate or Whatsoever sways this Earth.

Dying, his mangled body, to inter it,
He doth bequeath him into comrade hands;
His soul he renders to some Captain Spirit
That knows, admires, pities, and understands!

All this you knew by that which doth reside
Deeper than learning; by apprehension
Of ancient, dark, and melancholy pride
You were a Soldier true, and died as one.

All day the cold wind cries, the clouds unroll;
But to the cloud and wind I cry, 'Be still!'
What need of comfort has the heroic soul?
What soldier finds a soldier's grave is chill?

Anthem for Doomed Youth

WILFRED OWEN

What passing-bells for these who die as cattle?
   Only the monstrous anger of the guns.
   Only the stuttering rifles' rapid rattle
Can patter out their hasty orisons.*
No mockeries now for them; no prayers nor bells,
   Nor any voice of mourning save the choirs,—
The shrill demented choirs of wailing shells;
   And bugles calling for them from sad shires.

What candles may be held to speed them all?
   Not in the hands of boys, but in their eyes
Shall shine the holy glimmers of good-byes.
   The pallor of girls' brows shall be their pall;
Their flowers the tenderness of patient minds,
And each slow dusk a drawing-down of blinds.

* prayers.

At a Calvary near the Ancre

WILFRED OWEN

One ever hangs where shelled roads part.
  In this war He too lost a limb,
But His disciples hide apart;
  And now the Soldiers bear with Him.

Near Golgotha strolls many a priest,
  And in their faces there is pride
That they were flesh-marked by the Beast
  By whom the gentle Christ's denied.

The scribes on all the people shove
  And bawl allegiance to the state,
But they who love the greater love
  Lay down their life; they do not hate.

Futility

WILFRED OWEN

Move him into the sun—
Gently its touch awoke him once,
At home, whispering of fields unsown.
Always it woke him, even in France,
Until this morning and this snow.
If anything might rouse him now
The kind old sun will know.

Think how it wakes the seeds,—
Woke, once, the clays of a cold star.
Are limbs, so dear-achieved, are sides,
Full-nerved—still warm—too hard to stir?
Was it for this the clay grew tall?

—O what made fatuous sunbeams toil
To break earth's sleep at all?

The Next War

WILFRED OWEN

War's a joke for me and you,
While we know such dreams are true.
                 (Siegfried Sassoon)

Out there, we've walked quite friendly up to Death;
  Sat down and eaten with him, cool and bland,—
  Pardoned his spilling mess-tins in our hand.
We've sniffed the green thick odour of his breath,—
Our eyes wept, but our courage didn't writhe.
  He's spat at us with bullets and he's coughed
  Shrapnel. We chorussed when he sang aloft;
We whistled while he shaved us with his scythe.

Oh, Death was never enemy of ours!
  We laughed at him, we leagued with him, old chum.
No soldier's paid to kick against his powers.
  We laughed, knowing that better men would come,
And greater wars; when each proud fighter brags
He wars on Death—for Life; not men—for flags.

The Parable of the Old Man
and the Young

WILFRED OWEN

So Abram rose, and clave* the wood, and went,
And took the fire with him, and a knife.

* broke up.

98

And as they sojourned both of them together,
Isaac the first-born spake and said, My Father,
Behold the preparations, fire and iron,
But where the lamb for this burnt-offering?
Then Abram bound the youth with belts and straps,
And builded parapets and trenches there,
And stretchèd forth the knife to slay his son.
When lo! an angel called him out of heaven,
Saying, Lay not thy hand upon the lad,
Neither do anything to him. Behold,
A ram, caught in a thicket by its horns;
Offer the Ram of Pride instead of him.
But the old man would not so, but slew his son,
And half the seed of Europe, one by one.

The Send-Off

WILFRED OWEN

Down the close, darkening lanes they sang their way
To the siding-shed,
And lined the train with faces grimly gay.

Their breasts were stuck all white with wreath and
    spray
As men's are, dead.

Dull porters watched them, and a casual tramp
Stood staring hard,
Sorry to miss them from the upland camp.
Then, unmoved, signals nodded, and a lamp
Winked to the guard.

So secretly, like wrongs hushed-up, they went.
They were not ours:
We never heard to which front these were sent.

Nor there if they yet mock what women meant
Who gave them flowers.

Shall they return to beatings of great bells
In wild train-loads?
A few, a few, too few for drums and yells,
May creep back, silent, to still village wells
Up half-known roads.

Strange Meeting

WILFRED OWEN

It seemed that out of battle I escaped
Down some profound dull tunnel, long since scooped
Through granites which titanic wars had groined.
Yet also there encumbered sleepers groaned,
Too fast in thought or death to be bestirred.
Then, as I probed them, one sprang up, and stared
With piteous recognition in fixed eyes,
Lifting distressful hands as if to bless.
And by his smile, I knew that sullen hall,
By his dead smile I knew we stood in Hell.
With a thousand pains that vision's face was grained;
Yet no blood reached there from the upper ground,
And no guns thumped, or down the flues made moan.
'Strange friend,' I said, 'here is no cause to mourn.'
'None,' said that other, 'save the undone years,
The hopelessness. Whatever hope is yours,
Was my life also; I went hunting wild
After the wildest beauty in the world,
Which lies not calm in eyes, or braided hair,

But mocks the steady running of the hour,
And if it grieves, grieves richlier than here.
For my glee might many men have laughed,
And of my weeping something had been left,
Which must die now. I mean the truth untold,
The pity of war, the pity war distilled.
Now men will go content with what we spoiled,
Or, discontent, boil bloody, and be spilled.
They will be swift with swiftness of the tigress.
None will break ranks, though nations trek from
    progress.
Courage was mine, and I had mystery,
Wisdom was mine, and I had mastery;
To miss the march of this retreating world
Into vain citadels that are not walled.
Then, when much blood had clogged their chariot-
    wheels,
I would go up and wash them from sweet wells,
Even with truths that lie too deep for taint.
I would have poured my spirit without stint
But not through wounds; not on the cess of war.
Foreheads of men have bled where no wounds were.
I am the enemy you killed, my friend.
I knew you in this dark: for so you frowned
Yesterday through me as you jabbed and killed.
I parried; but my hands were loath and cold.
Let us sleep now. . . .'

Three Hills

EVERARD OWEN

There is a hill in England,
    Green fields and a school* I know,

* Harrow School.

Where the balls fly fast in summer,
  And the whispering elm-trees grow,
    A little hill, a dear hill,
  And the playing fields below.

There is a hill* in Flanders,
  Heaped with a thousand slain,
Where the shells fly night and noontide
  And the ghosts that died in vain,
    A little hill, a hard hill
  To the souls that died in pain.

There is a hill† in Jewry,
  Three crosses pierce the sky,
On the midmost He is dying
  To save all those who die,
    A little hill, a kind hill
  To souls in jeopardy.

Air Raid: 1917–18

HERBERT PALMER

I wonder if they'll come tonight!
The round moon rolls in silvery light,
No sound throbs on the windless air.

For, though I tremble to confess,
I never feel more cheerfulness
Than when the German raiders fly
Like bees across the cloudless sky.
And neither pity, pain, nor terror
Will ever wean me from my error.

* Hill 60.   † Calvary.

For oh, to hear the mad guns go,
And watch the starry night aglow
With radiance of crackling fires
And the white searchlights' quivering spires!
For sure, such splendour doth assuage
The very cannon of its rage!

My neighbour plays a violin,
Shedding sweet silver down the din
And songs for fears to dwindle in.

But the houses shake: and the dogs wake.
They growl, they bark for warrior joy,
And seek the airmen to annoy.

Up go their tails into the air,
They gnash their teeth, and their eyes glare.
But on those cruel raiders sail,
Regardless of each quivering tail.

And one gun has a booming note,
Another has a cold in throat;
And some are mellow, and some hoarse,
And some sound sobbing with remorse;
Quite four or five ring musical,
And others very keen to kill.

You'd say that twenty champagne corks
Were popping in the London walks.
You'd say that drunken men in scores
Were smashing glass and slamming doors.
You'd say a twanging banjo string
Had snapped in twain from hammering.
You'd say that wild orchestral fellows
Were banging God's Throne with their 'cellos.

A wail, a crash, like steel trays falling.
And a wind upon the Common, calling.

And over us a sound of humming
—Of hornets or bad bees a-bumming!
A devilish, strident, hoarse, discordant
Whirring of dark fliers mordant.
My soul stands still and sweats with fear.

But the Heavenly stars, all shimmering,
Dance in a giddy whirl and sing.
And other stars of the Earth, shake sheer
From the mouths of the black guns thundering.

'Tis like some ruining harmony
I heard in Berlin on the Spree
The day they played the *Valkyrie*.*

Kind Heaven will comfort my wracked wits
Before I'm blown to little bits.

Germania

EDEN PHILLPOTTS

Surgeon her world! Let myriad scalpels bright
Flash in her sores with all thy bitter might,
    So that their aching cease.
Cut clean the cursed canker that doth foul
Her spirit; tent and cleanse her sorry soul,
    And give her bosom peace.

* Wagner's opera, *Die Walküre*.

We do not smite a nation, but a pest;
Humanity makes reasonable quest
    To free a noble slave.
Full deep she groans and faints, and fainting feels
Archaic torture of a tyrant's heels
    Grinding her to her grave.

Possessed of devils now, mad with her woes,
She wounds the world and turns her friends to foes;
    But cast her devils down
And broken, humbled, contrite, healed and sane
Oh may she shine her glorious self again—
    Pearl in Europa's crown.

And they accurs'd, who bred this in her heart,
Shall from the councils of mankind depart,
    While over sea and shore,
The silver trumpets of the sunrise cry
That earth pursue her solemn destiny
    By blood and iron no more.

When it's Over

MAX PLOWMAN

'Young soldier, what will you be
    When it's all over?'
'I shall get out and across the sea,
Where land's cheap and a man can thrive.
I shall make money. Perhaps I'll wive
In a place where there's room for a family.
    I'm a bit of a rover.'

'Young soldier, what will you be
    At the last "Dismiss"?'

'Bucked to get back to old Leicester Square,
Where there's good champagne and a glad eye
          winking,
And no more "Verey Lights" damnably blinking
Their weary, dreary, white-eyed stare.
     I'll be out of this.'

'Young soldier, what will you be
     When they sign the peace?'
'Blowed if I know; perhaps I shall stick it.
The job's all right if you take it steady.
After all, somebody's got to be ready,
And tons of the blighters 'll get their ticket.
     War's don't cease.'

'Young soldier, what will you be
     At the day's end?'
'Tired's what I'll be. I shall lie on the beach
Of a shore where the rippling waves just sigh,
And listen and dream and sleep and lie
Forgetting what I've had to learn and teach
     And attack and defend.'

'Young soldier, what will you be
     When you're next a-bed?'
'God knows what; but it doesn't matter,
For whenever I think, I always remember
The Belgians massacred that September,
And England's pledge—and the rest seems chatter.
     What if I *am* dead?'

'Young soldier, what will you be
     When it's all done?'
'I shall come back and live alone
On an English farm in the Sussex Weald,

Where the wounds in my mind will be slowly sealed,
And the graves in my heart will be overgrown;
　　And I'll sit in the sun.'

'Young soldier, what will you be
　　At the "Last Post"?'
'Cold, cold in the tender earth,
A cold body in foreign soil;
But a happy spirit fate can't spoil,
And an extra note in the blackbird's mirth
　　From a khaki ghost.'

The Happy Warrior

HERBERT READ

His wild heart beats with painful sobs,
His strained hands clench as ice-cold rifle,
His aching jaws grip a hot parched tongue,
His wide eyes search unconsciously.

He cannot shriek.

Bloody saliva
Dribbles down his shapeless jacket.

I saw him stab
And stab again
A well-killed Boche.

This is the happy warrior,
This is he. . . .

from 'My Company'

HERBERT READ

I

You became
In many acts and quiet observances
A body and a soul, entire.

I cannot tell
What time your life became mine:
Perhaps when one summer night
We halted on the roadside
In the starlight only,
And you sang your sad home-songs,
Dirges which I standing outside you
Coldly condemned.

Perhaps, one night, descending cold
When rum was mighty acceptable,
And my doling gave birth to sensual gratitude.

And then our fights; we've fought together
Compact, unanimous;
And I have felt the pride of leadership.

In many acts and quiet observances
You absorbed me:
Until one day I stood eminent
And I saw you gathered round me,
Uplooking,
And about you a radiance that seemed to beat
With variant glow and to give
Grace to our unity.

But, God! I know that I'll stand
Someday in the loneliest wilderness,
Someday my heart will cry
For the soul that has been, but that now
Is scattered with the winds,
Deceased and devoid.

I know that I'll wander with a cry:
'O beautiful men, O men I loved,
O whither are you gone, my company?'

from 'Kneeshaw goes to War'

HERBERT READ

IV

There are a few left who will find it hard to forget
Polygonveld.
The earth was scarred and broken
By torrents of plunging shells;
Then washed and sodden with autumnal rains.
And Polygonbeke
(Perhaps a rippling stream
In the days of Kneeshaw's gloom)
Spread itself like a fatal quicksand,
A sucking, clutching death.
They had to be across the beke
And in their line before dawn.
A man who was marching by Kneeshaw's side
Hesitated in the middle of the mud,
And slowly sank, weighted down by equipment
    and arms.
He cried for help;

Rifles were stretched to him;
He clutched and they tugged,
But slowly he sank.
His terror grew—
Grew visibly when the viscous ooze.
Reached his neck.
And there he seemed to stick,
Sinking no more.
They could not dig him out—
The oozing mud would flow back again.

The dawn was very near.

An officer shot him through the head:
Not a neat job—the revolver
Was too close.

V

Then the dawn came, silver on the wet brown
    earth.

Kneeshaw found himself in the second wave:
The unseen springs revolved the cog
Through all the mutations of that storm of
    death.
He started when he heard them cry 'Dig in!'
He had to think and couldn't for a while.
Then he seized a pick from the nearest man
And clawed passionately upon the churned
    earth.
With satisfaction his pick
Cleft the skull of a buried man.
Kneeshaw tugged the clinging pick,
Saw its burden and shrieked.

For a second or two he was impotent
Vainly trying to recover his will, but his senses
    prevailing.

Then mercifully
A hot blast and riotous detonation
Hurled his mangled body
Into the beautiful peace of coma.

Ypres

HERBERT READ

With a dull and hazy light
    the sun of a winter noon
        swills
            thy ruins,
Thy ruins etched
    in silver silhouettes
        against a turquoise sky.
Lank poles leap to the infinite,
    their broken wires
        tossed like the rat-locks of Maenades.
And Desolation broods over all,
    gathering to her lap
        her leprous children.
The sparrows whimper
    amid the broken arches.

The Soldier Addresses His Body

EDGELL RICKWORD

I shall be mad if you get smashed about;
we've had good times together, you and I;

although you groused a bit when luck was out,
and a girl turned us down, or we went dry.

Yet there's a world of things we haven't done,
countries not seen, where people do strange
   things;
eat fish alive, and mimic in the sun
the solemn gestures of their stone-grey kings.

I've heard of forests that are dim at noon
where snakes and creepers wrestle all day long;
where vivid beasts grow pale with the full moon,
gibber and cry, and wail a mad old song;

because at the full moon the Hippogriff*
with crinkled ivory snout and agate feet,
with his green eye will glare them cold and stiff
for the coward Wyvern* to come down and eat.

Vodka and kvass,† and bitter mountain wines
we've never drunk, nor snatched at bursting grapes
to pelt slim girls among Sicilian vines,
who'd flicker through the leaves, faint frolic shapes.

Yes, there are many things we have not done,
but it's a sweat to knock them into rhyme,
let's have a drink, and give the cards a run
and leave dull verse to the dull peaceful time:

Trench Poets

EDGELL RICKWORD

I knew a man, he was my chum,
but he grew blacker every day,

* legendary animals.   † Russian drinks.

and would not brush the flies away,
nor blanch however fierce the hum
of passing shells; I used to read,
to rouse him, random things from Donne—
like 'Get with child a mandrake-root.'
But you can tell he was far gone,
for he lay gaping, mackerel-eyed,
and stiff and senseless as a post
even when that old poet cried
'I long to talk with some old lover's ghost.'

I tried the Elegies* one day,
but he, because he heard me say:
'What needst thou have more covering than a
    man?'
grinned nastily, and so I knew
the worms had got his brains at last.
There was one thing that I might do
To starve the worms; I racked my head
for healthy things and quoted *Maud.*†
His grin got worse and I could see
he sneered at passion's purity.
He stank so badly, though we were great chums
I had to leave him; then rats ate his thumbs.

War and Peace

EDGELL RICKWORD

In sodden trenches I have heard men speak,
though numb and wretched, wise and witty things;
and loved them for the stubbornness that clings
longest to laughter when Death's pulleys creak;

* Donne's most erotic poems.   † Tennyson's poem.

and seeing cool nurses move on tireless feet
to do abominable things with grace,
dreamed them sweet sisters in that haunted place
where with child voices strong men howl or bleat.

Yet now those men lay stubborn courage by,
riding dull-eyed and silent in the train
to old men's stools; or sell gay-coloured socks
and listen fearfully for Death; so I
love the low-laughing girls, who now again
go daintily, in thin and flowery frocks.

Winter Warfare

EDGELL RICKWORD

Colonel Cold strode up the Line
    (Tabs of rime* and spurs of ice),
Stiffened all where he did glare,
    Horses, men, and lice.

Visited a forward post,
    Left them burning, ear to foot;
Fingers stuck to biting steel,
    Toes to frozen boot.

Stalked on into No Man's Land,
    Turned the wire to fleecy wool,
Iron stakes to sugar sticks
    Snapping at a pull.

Those who watched with hoary eyes
    Saw two figures gleaming there;
Hauptman Kälte, Colonel Cold,
    Gaunt, in the grey air.

* hoar frost.

Stiffly, tinkling spurs they moved,
   Glassy eyed, with glinting heel
Stabbing those who lingered there
   Torn by screaming steel.

Break of Day in the Trenches

ISAAC ROSENBERG

The darkness crumbles away—
It is the same old druid Time as ever.
Only a live thing leaps my hand—
A queer sardonic rat—
As I pull the parapet's poppy
To stick behind my ear.
Droll rat, they would shoot you if they knew
Your cosmopolitan sympathies
(And God knows what antipathies).
Now you have touched this English hand
You will do the same to a German—
Soon, no doubt, if it be your pleasure
To cross the sleeping green between.
It seems you inwardly grin as you pass
Strong eyes, fine limbs, haughty athletes
Less chanced than you for life,
Bonds to the whims of murder,
Sprawled in the bowels of the earth,
The torn fields of France.
What do you see in our eyes
At the shrieking iron and flame
Hurled through still heavens?
What quaver—what heart aghast?
Poppies whose roots are in man's veins
Drop, and are ever dropping;
But mine in my ear is safe,
Just a little white with the dust.

Dead Man's Dump

ISAAC ROSENBERG

The plunging limbers* over the shattered track
Racketed with their rusty freight,
Stuck out like many crowns of thorns,
And the rusty stakes like sceptres old
To stay the flood of brutish men
Upon our brothers dear.

The wheels lurched over sprawled dead
But pain them not, though their bones crunched;
Their shut mouths made no moan.
They lie there huddled, friend and foeman,
Man born of man, and born of woman;
And shells go crying over them
From night till night and now.

Earth has waited for them,
All the time of their growth
Fretting for their decay:
Now she has them at last!
In the strength of their strength
Suspended—stopped and held.

What fierce imaginings their dark souls lit?
Earth! Have they gone into you?
Somewhere they must have gone,
And flung on your hard back
Is their soul's sack,
Emptied of God-ancestralled essences.
Who hurled them out? Who hurled?

* two-wheeled carts.

None saw their spirits' shadow shake the grass,
Or stood aside for the half used life to pass
Out of those doomed nostrils and the doomed
  mouth,
When the swift iron burning bee
Drained the wild honey of their youth.

What of us who, flung on the shrieking pyre,
Walk, our usual thoughts untouched,
Our lucky limbs as on ichor* fed,
Immortal seeming ever?
Perhaps when the flames beat loud on us,
A fear may choke in our veins
And the startled blood may stop.
The air is loud with death,
The dark air spurts with fire,
The explosions ceaseless are.
Timelessly now, some minutes past,
These dead strode time with vigorous life,
Till the shrapnel called 'An end!'
But not to all. In bleeding pangs
Some borne on stretchers dreamed of home,
Dear things, war-blotted from their hearts.

A man's brains splattered on
A stretcher-bearer's face:
His shook shoulders slipped their load,
But when they bent to look again
The drowning soul was sunk too deep
For human tenderness.

They left this dead with the older dead,
Stretched at the cross roads.

* divine fluid.

Burnt black by strange decay
Their sinister faces lie,
The lid over each eye;
The grass and coloured clay
More motion have than they,
Joined to the great sunk silences.

Here is one not long dead.
His dark hearing caught our far wheels,
And the choked soul stretched weak hands
To reach the living world the far wheels said;
The blood-dazed intelligence beating for light,
Crying through the suspense of the far-torturing
    wheels
Swift for the end to break
Or the wheels to break,
Cried as the tick of the world broke over his
    sight,
'Will they come? Will they ever come?'
Even as the mixed hoofs of the mules,
The quivering-bellied mules,
And the rushing wheels all mixed
With his tortured upturned sight.

So we crashed round the bend,
We heard his weak scream,
We heard his very last sound,
And our wheels grazed his dead face.

Louse Hunting

ISAAC ROSENBERG

Nudes, stark and glistening,
Yelling in lurid glee. Grinning faces

And raging limbs
Whirl over the floor on fire.
For a shirt verminously busy
Yon soldier tore from his throat
With oaths
Godhead might shrink at, but not the lice.
And soon the shirt was aflare
Over the candle he'd lit while we lay.

Then we all sprang up and stript
To hunt the verminous brood.
Soon like a demons' pantomime
This plunge was raging.
See the silhouettes agape,
See the gibbering shadows
Mixed with the baffled arms on the wall.
See gargantuan hooked fingers
Pluck in supreme flesh
To smutch* supreme littleness.
See the merry limbs in that Highland fling
Because some wizard vermin
Charmed from the quiet this revel
When our ears were half-lulled
By the dark music
Blown from Sleep's trumpet.

Marching

As seen from the Left File

ISAAC ROSENBERG

My eyes catch ruddy necks
Sturdily pressed back—

* stain.

All a red brick moving glint.
Like flaming pendulums, hands
Swing across the khaki—
Mustard-coloured khaki—
To the automatic feet.

We husband the ancient glory
In these bared necks and hands.
Not broke is the forge of Mars;
But a subtler brain beats iron
To shoe the hoofs of death
(Who paws dynamic air now).
Blind fingers loose on iron cloud
To rain immortal darkness
On strong eyes.

The General

SIEGFRIED SASSOON

'Good-morning; good-morning!' the General said
When we met him last week on our way to the line.
Now the soldiers he smiled at are most of 'em dead,
And we're cursing his staff for incompetent swine.
'He's a cheery old card,' grunted Harry to Jack
As they slogged up to Arras with rifle and pack.

But he did for them both by his plan of attack.

Counter-Attack

SIEGFRIED SASSOON

We'd gained our first objective hours before
While dawn broke like a face with blinking eyes,

Pallid, unshaved and thirsty, blind with smoke.
Things seemed all right at first. We held their line,
With bombers posted, Lewis guns well placed,
And clink of shovels deepening the shallow trench.
  The place was rotten with dead; green clumsy legs
  High-booted, sprawled and grovelled along the saps
  And trunks, face downward, in the sucking mud,
  Wallowed like trodden sand-bags loosely filled;
  And naked sodden buttocks, mats of hair,
  Bulged, clotted heads slept in the plastering slime.
  And then the rain began,—the jolly old rain!

A yawning soldier knelt against the bank,
Staring across the morning blear with fog;
He wondered when the Allemands* would get busy;
And then, of course, they started with five-nines
Traversing, sure as fate, and never a dud.
Mute in the clamour of shells he watched them burst
Spouting dark earth and wire with gusts from hell,
While posturing giants dissolved in drifts of smoke.
He crouched and flinched, dizzy with galloping fear,
Sick for escape,—loathing the strangled horror
And butchered, frantic gestures of the dead.

An officer came blundering down the trench:
'Stand-to and man the fire-step!' On he went . . .
Gasping and bawling, 'Fire-step . . . counter-attack!'
  Then the haze lifted. Bombing on the right
  Down the old sap: machine-guns on the left;
  And stumbling figures looming out in front.
  'O Christ, they're coming at us!' Bullets spat,
And he remembered his rifle . . . rapid fire . . .
And started blazing wildly . . . then a bang
Crumpled and spun him sideways, knocked him out

* Germans.

121

To grunt and wriggle: none heeded him; he chocked
And fought the flapping veils of smothering gloom,
Lost in a blurred confusion of yells and groans ...
Down, and down, and down, he sank and drowned,
Bleeding to death. The counter-attack had failed.

Does it Matter?

SIEGFRIED SASSOON

Does it matter?—losing your legs? ...
For people will always be kind,
And you need not show that you mind
When the others come in after hunting
To gobble their muffins and eggs.

Does it matter?—losing your sight? ...
There's such splendid work for the blind;
And people will always be kind,
As you sit on the terrace remembering
And turning your face to the light.

Do they matter?—those dreams from the pit? ...
You can drink and forget and be glad,
And people won't say that you're mad,
For they'll know you've fought for your
      country
And no one will worry a bit.

The Dug-Out

SIEGFRIED SASSOON

Why do you lie with your legs ungainly huddled,
And one arm bent across your sullen, cold,

Exhausted face? It hurts my heart to watch you,
Deep-shadow'd from the candle's guttering gold;
And you wonder why I shake you by the shoulder;
Drowsy, you mumble and sigh and turn your head . . .
You are too young to fall asleep for ever;
And when you sleep you remind me of the dead.

Lamentations

SIEGFRIED SASSOON

I found him in the guard-room at the Base.
From the blind darkness I had heard his crying
And blundered in. With puzzled, patient face
A sergeant watched him; it is no good trying
To stop it; for he howled and beat his chest.
And, all because his brother had gone west,
Raved at the bleeding war; his rampant grief
Moaned, shouted, sobbed, and choked, while
    he was kneeling
Half-naked on the floor. In my belief
Such men have lost all patriotic feeling.

Stretcher Case

SIEGFRIED SASSOON

He woke; the clank and racket of the train
Kept time with angry throbbings in his brain.
Then for a while he lapsed and drowsed again.
At last he lifted his bewildered eyes
And blinked, and rolled them sidelong; hills and
    skies,

Heavily wooded, hot with August haze,
And, slipping backward, golden for his gaze,
Acres of harvest.

           Feebly now he drags
Exhausted ego back from glooms and quags
And blasting tumult, terror, hurtling glare,
To calm and brightness, havens of sweet air.
He sighed, confused; then drew a cautious breath;
This level journeying was no ride through death.
'If I were dead,' he mused, 'there'd be no thinking—
Only some plunging underworld of sinking,
And hueless, shifting welter where I'd drown.'

Then he remembered that his name was Brown.

But was he back in Blighty? Slow he turned,
Till in his heart thanksgiving leapt and burned.
There shone the blue serene, the prosperous land,
Trees, cows and hedges; skipping these, he scanned
Large, friendly names, that change not with the year,
Lung Tonic, Mustard, Liver Pills and Beer.

The Rear-Guard

Hindenburg Line, April 1917

SIEGFRIED SASSOON

Groping along the tunnel, step by step,
He winked his prying torch with patching glare
From side to side, and sniffed the unwholesome air.
Tins, boxes, bottles, shapes too vague to know;
A mirror smashed, the mattress from a bed;

And he, exploring fifty feet below
The rosy gloom of battle overhead.

Tripping, he grabbed the wall; saw someone lie
Humped at his feet, half-hidden by a rug,
And stooped to give the sleeper's arm a tug.
'I'm looking for headquarters.' No reply.
'God blast your neck!' (For days he'd had no sleep,)
'Get up and guide me through this stinking place.'

Savage, he kicked a soft, unanswering heap,
And flashed his beam across the livid face
Terribly glaring up, whose eyes yet wore
Agony dying hard ten days before;
And fists of fingers clutched a blackening wound

Alone he staggered on until he found
Dawn's ghost that filtered down a shafted stair
To the dazed, muttering creatures underground
Who hear the boom of shells in muffled sound.
At last, with sweat of horror in his hair,
He climbed through darkness to the twilight air,
Unloading hell behind him step by step.

Judas and the Profiteer

OSBERT SITWELL

Judas descended to his lower Hell
   To meet his only friend—the profiteer—
Who, looking fat and rubicund and well,
   Regarded him, and then said with a sneer,
'Iscariot, they did you! Fool! to sell
   For silver pence the body of God's Son,

Whereas for maiming men with sword and shell
　　I gain at least a golden million.'

But Judas answered: 'You deserve your gold;
　　It's not His body but His soul you've sold!'

The Modern Abraham

OSBERT SITWELL
(*To Siegfried Sassoon*)

His purple fingers clutch a large cigar—
　　Plump, mottled fingers, with a ring or two.
He rests back in his fat armchair. The war
　　Has made this change in him. As he looks through
His cheque-book with a tragic look he sighs:
　　'Disabled Soldiers' Fund' he reads afresh,
And through his meat-red face peer angry eyes—
　　The spirit piercing through its mound of flesh.

They should not ask me to subscribe again!
　　Consider me and all that I have done—
I've fought for Britain with my might and main;
　　I make explosives—and I gave a son.
My factory, converted for the fight
　　(I do not like to boast of what I've spent),
Now manufactures gas and dynamite,
　　Which only pays me seventy per cent.
And if I had ten other sons to send
I'd make them serve my country to the end,
So all the neighbours should flock round and say:
　　'Oh! look what Mr. Abraham has done.
He loves his country in the elder way;
　　Poor gentleman, he's lost another son!'

'When You See Millions
of the Mouthless Dead'

C. H. SORLEY

When you see millions of the mouthless dead
Across your dreams in pale battalions go,
Say not soft things as other man have said,
That you'll remember. For you need not so.
Give them not praise. For, deaf, how should they know
It is not curses heaped on each gashed head?
Nor tears. The blind eyes see not your tears flow.
Nor honour. It is easy to be dead.
Say only this, 'They are dead.' Then add thereto,
'Yet many a better one has died before.'
Then, scanning all the o'ercrowded mass, should you
Perceive one face that you loved heretofore,
It is a spook. None wears the face you knew.
Great death has made all his for evermore.

To Germany

C. H. SORLEY

You are blind like us. Your hurt no man designed,
And no man claimed the conquest of your land.
But gropers both through fields of thought confined
We stumble and we do not understand.
You only saw your future bigly planned,
And we, the tapering paths of our own mind,
And in each other's dearest ways we stand,
And hiss and hate. And the blind fight the blind.

When it is peace, then we may view again
With new-won eyes each other's truer form

And wonder. Grown more loving-kind and warm
We'll grasp firm hands and laugh at the old pain,
When it is peace. But until peace, the storm
The darkness and the thunder and the rain.

'All the hills and vales along'

C. H. SORLEY

All the hills and vales along
Earth is bursting into song,
And the singers are the chaps
Who are going to die perhaps.
    O sing, marching men,
    Till the valleys ring again.
    Give your gladness to earth's keeping,
    So be glad when you are sleeping.

Cast away regret and rue,
Think what they are marching to,
Little give, great pass.
Jesus Christ and Barabbas
Were found the same day.
This died, that went his way.
    So sing with joyful breath.
    For why, you are going to death.
    Teeming earth will surely store
    All the gladness that you pour.

Earth that never doubts nor fears
Earth that knows of death, not tears,
Earth that bore with joyful ease
Hemlock for Socrates,

Earth that blossomed and was glad
'Neath the cross that Christ had,
Shall rejoice and blossom too
When the bullet reaches you.
  Wherefore, men marching
  On the road to death, sing!
  Pour gladness on earth's head,
  So be merry, so be dead.

From the hills and valleys earth
Shouts back the sound of mirth,
Tramp of feet and lilt of song
Ringing all the road along.
All the music of their going,
Ringing swinging glad song-throwing,
Earth will echo still, when foot
Lies numb and voice mute.
  On marching men, on
  To the gates of death with song.
  Sow your gladness for earth's reaping,
  So you may be glad though sleeping.
  Strew your gladness on earth's bed,
  So be merry, so be dead.

Home Thoughts in Laventie

E. W. TENNANT

Green gardens in Laventie!
Soldiers only know the street
Where the mud is churned and splashed about
  By battle-wending feet;
And yet beside one stricken house there is a glimpse of grass.
  Look for it when you pass.

Beyond the church whose pitted spire
Seems balanced on a strand
Of swaying stone and tottering brick
Two roofless ruins stand,
And here behind the wreckage where the back wall should have
been
We found a garden green.

The grass was never trodden on,
The little path of gravel
Was overgrown with celandine,
No other folk did travel
Along its weedy surface, but the nimble-footed mouse
Running from house to house.

So all among the vivid blades
Of soft and tender grass
We lay, nor heard the limber* wheels
That pass and ever pass,
In noisy continuity until their very rattle
Seems in itself a battle.

At length we rose up from this ease
Of tranquil happy mind,
And searched the garden's little length
A fresh pleasaunce to find;
And there some yellow daffodils and jasmine hanging high
Did rest the tired eye.

The fairest and most fragrant
Of the many sweets we found,
Was a little bush of daphne flower
Upon a grassy mound,
And so thick were the blossoms set and so divine the scent
That we were well content.

* cart.

Hungry for spring, I bent my head,
The perfume fanned my face,
And all my soul was dancing
In that lovely little place,
Dancing with a measured step from wrecked and shattered
towns
Away upon the Downs.

I saw green banks of daffodil,
Slim poplars in the breeze,
Great tan-brown hares in gusty March
A-courting on the leas;
And meadows with their glittering streams, and silver scurry-
ing dace,
Home—what a perfect place!

A Private

EDWARD THOMAS

This ploughman dead in battle slept out of doors
Many a frozen night, and merrily
Answered staid drinkers, good bedmen, and all bores:
'At Mrs. Greenland's Hawthorn Bush', said he,
'I slept.' None knew which bush. Above the town,
Beyond 'The Drover', a hundred spot the down
In Wiltshire. And where now at last he sleeps
More sound in France—that, too, he secret keeps.

Lights Out

EDWARD THOMAS

I have come to the borders of sleep,
The unfathomable deep

Forest where all must lose
Their way, however straight,
Or winding, soon or late;
They cannot chose.

Many a road and track
That, since the dawn's first crack,
Up to the forest brink,
Deceived the travellers,
Suddenly now blurs,
And in they sink.

Here love ends,
Despair, ambition ends;
All pleasure and all trouble,
Although most sweet or bitter,
Here ends in sleep that is sweeter
Than tasks most noble

There is not any book
Or face of dearest look
That I would not turn from now
To go into the unknown
I must enter, and leave, alone,
I know not how.

The tall forest towers;
Its cloudy foliage lowers
Ahead, shelf above shelf;
Its silence I hear and obey
That I may lose my way
And myself.

No One Cares Less Than I

EDWARD THOMAS

'No one cares less than I,
Nobody knows but God,
Whether I am destined to lie
Under a foreign clod,'
Were the words I made to the bugle
   call in the morning.

But laughing, storming, scorning,
Only the bugles know
What the bugles say in the morning,
And they do not care, when they blow
The call that I heard and made words to
   early this morning.

The Trumpet

EDWARD THOMAS

Rise up, rise up,
And as the trumpet blowing
Chases the dreams of men,
As the dawn glowing
The stars that left unlit
The land and water,
Rise up and scatter
That dew that covers
The print of last night's lovers—
Scatter it, scatter it!

While you are listening
To the clear horn,

Forget, men, everything
On this earth new-born,
Except that it is lovelier
Than any mysteries.
Open your eyes to the air
That has washed the eyes of the stars
Through all the dewy night:
Up with the light,
To the old wars;
Arise, arise!

Advance on the Somme

HERBERT TRENCH

I

Wild airman, you, the battle's eyes,
   Who, hovering over forest air,
Can every belt of cloud despise
   And through them fall without despair,
No cannon's sound to you can rise.
    But, say, how goes the battle there,
      As they advance?

II

Be dumb, choked heart! for they are dumb—
   Our men advancing. All's at stake!
The woods are bullet-stript—with hum
   Of cannon all the pastures shake;
And some will cross the crest, and some
   Will halt for ever in the brake,
      As they advance.

III

The ground is bubbling—pit and mire—
  And blackened with the blood of sons.
Death rains on every yard; and fire
  Shuttles the veil with woof of guns.
Dread is flag those weavers dire
  Unroll to shroud our gallant ones
    As they advance!

IV

They followed once—who rode so well—
  As brave a hunt as e'er blew horn:
And now through warren'd woods of hell
  They follow till the fateful morn.
And them the mudstain'd sentinel
  Shall watch, and see an age newborn
    As they advance!

from 'Battle of the Marne'

HERBERT TRENCH

XIII

Four nights along the marshy zone of mists
The sleepless line of France resists;
And four nights end those days
With apocalyptic blaze,
Uncertain darkness shot with rays,
And golden smoke
Rolls out over the thick reeds
Deepening the mystery of those dead waters.
The eyeless Château Mondement,
Towering and hollow guard,

That like another Lear
Stands at the marshes' end and narrow gate,
Upon his bosky mountain spur
By Poirier's hill white-scarr'd—
Besieged and lost
By either host,
Lighteth no more for the marsh-wanderer
Upon his naked-rafter'd turret spire,
The kindly signal fire
That he for centuries was wont to raise.
Summon'd in vain to be strife's arbiter
He with insane dark gaze
Nightlong upon his plateau listens
Smitten with gun on gun,
And feels beneath his trembling woods,
And about his deep-ravined and dusky base,
The arms of great and little Morin run
Thrilled with the fate of all that they embrace.

XIV

Four nights doth parching battle sway
Towards the fourth inexorable day;
Then outbreaks autumn tempest, rain and hail
Towards evening of the day.
And, with the rising of that sunset gale,
When at last the long-awaited Forty-second
Division rode down to Corroy
Everywhere then came leapings of the heart!
Whisperers strange upstart,
Leaf-hosts in whirl'd careers
Down Marne's cliffs, willow'd reaches, swollen
   weirs,
Over the bridge of Lagny's foundered piers
And St Rémy's cannon-lighted heart;

From vineyard, marsh, heath, copse,
Caught up to mix above the forest tops,
And blazon'd on a hundred winds to dance
Upon the glowing misty airs
With low and feverish cries
Whirls the whole realm of leaves.
And the young men, lifting up their fierce
    exhausted eyes
Above the woods of Gault and forests of
    Traonne,
And from the seven poplar'd roads
Threading the marshland zone,
Behold the voyage of those torn leaves
And, launched above their spiral rise
Out of all her deep and stubborn families,
They see ascend the wingèd feet of France
Terribly to repel.
'Behold her,' cry the leaves, and winds eternal
'Thrice holy, the maternal,
Thrice holy, the son-shaper,
Herself our radiant eddy of star vapour
Out of whirlwinds of the planet, plant and shell,
Emerging to repair her wounded cell.'
They remember her, red leaves, and with no
    fears.
Not in the day serene,
In cities of the vintage proud,
Plainly by them was this Immortal seen,
But now, against the midnight thunder-cloud,
Above the shell-pits of our field of dead.
Her lineaments are clear, devoid of dread,
The glories of her wings are bow'd
To us, when our light fails
And to the inconsolable her face unveils.
The soul of one called France—

A secret spirit—far
Stronger than any France—
Hath turned the tide of war
And baulk'd the great advance
Of yonder cannoniers.

Aeroplanes

W. J. TURNER

Iron birds floating in the sky
   Prey remorselessly
On the tiny, obscure dot
That is some great city,
Below, men-insects rend and tear,
Women wring hands of pity.

I have flown a hundred miles
   Over the blurred plain,
Dropping devastation and death,
   Blotting men's nerves with pain—
Their miserable cries were as tiny as insects'
   Calling their God in vain.

The sounds of their oaths and lamentations
   Could not even reach up to me,
The clouds were at peace, no tribulation
   Disturbed the sky-harmony,
Only my buzzing engine clanged
   And my heart beat dreadfully.

I laughed as I silently tossed blind Death
   Down on that insect people,

Dreadful it was in the peaceful sky
  To murder that insect people,
And never to hear a sound or cry
  Or a bell toll in a steeple.

I laughed when my last bloody bomb had gone,
  I shrieked high up in a cloud,
I wanted to fly in the face of their God
  And spit my disdain aloud,
I ripped through the terrified whistling air
  And burst through the earth's damp shroud.

Ah! it was blue there, wide and clear,
  Dancing alive in the sun,
Amd millions of bright, swect cymbals rang
  Praising the deeds I had done,
And millions of angels cheering stood
  Deep-columned around the Sun.

And then I stood erect and cheered,
  Ay! shouted into the sky,
I filled the vast semicircle round
  There was only the Sun and I,
The round, red, glittering, blazing Sun
  And a fluttering human fly.

The Call

R. E. VERNÈDE

Lad, with the merry smile and the eyes
  Quick as a hawk's and clear as the day,
You who have counted the game the prize,
  Here is the game of games to play.

Never a goal—the captains say—
Matches the one that's needed now:
　　Put the old blazer and cap away—
England's colours await your brow.

Man, with the square-set jaws and chin,
　　Always, it seems, you have moved to your end
Sure of yourself, intent to win
　　Fame and wealth and the power to bend—
　　All that you've made you're called to spend,
All that you've sought you're asked to miss—
　　What's ambition compared with this
That a man lay down his life for his friend?

Dreamer, oft in your glancing mind
　　Brave with drinking the faerie brew,
You have smitten the ogres blind
　　When the fair Princess cried out to you.
　　Dreamer, what if your dreams are true?
Yonder's a bayonet, magical, since
　　Him whom it strikes, the blade sinks through—
Take it and strike for England, Prince!

Friend with the face so hard and worn,
　　The devil and you have sometime met,
And now you curse the day you were born,
　　And want one boon of God—to forget.
　　Ah, but I know, and yet—and yet—
I think, out there in the shrapnel spray,
　　You shall stand up and not regret
The Life that gave so splendid a day.

Lover of ease, you've lolled and forgot
　　All the things that you meant to right;
Life has been soft for you, has it not?

What offer does England make to-night?
    This—to toil and to march and to fight
As never you've dreamed since your life began;
    This—to carry the steel-swept height,
This—to know that you've played the man!

Brothers, brothers, the time is short,
    Nor soon again shall it so betide
That a man may pass from the common sort
    Sudden and stand by the heroes' side.
    Are there some that being named yet bide?—
Hark once more to the clarion call—
    Sounded by him who deathless died—
'This day England expects you all.'

Sons of Britain

WILLIAM WATSON

Sons of her who keeps her faith unbroken,
    Her who gave you might of limb and nerve,
Her whose service—be it devoutly spoken—
    Perfect freedom is, for all who serve:

Her who gave you dower of iron sinew,
    Her who made you strong and fleet and brave—
Give her all the manhood that is in you:
    'Tis the royal gift her own hands gave.

England's safety—England's dearer honour—
    Both forbid that you should halt and wait
Till the enemy be indeed upon her,
    He who vaunts and flaunts him at her gate.

Heed not overmuch when she is slandered;
   Yours to guard her from a Bully's blow:
Yours to rise, and rally to her standard:
   Yours to arm, and face the brutal foe.

Would you sit at home, and watch and ponder,
   While the warriors agonise and dare?
Here for you is shame, but glory yonder:
   Choose the glory—yea, a hero's share.

Then, though darksome be the hour, and grievous,
   You shall make it great and splendid too,
And her love who bore and did conceive us
   Shall for ever crown your deeds and you.

God, How I Hate You

ARTHUR GRAEME WEST

God! how I hate you, you young cheerful men,
Whose pious poetry blossoms on your graves
As soon as you are in them . . .
                       Hark how one chants—
'Oh happy to have lived these epic days'—
'These epic days'! And *he'd* been to France,
And seen the trenches, glimpsed the huddled dead
In the periscope, hung on the rusty wire:
Choked by their sickly foetor,* day and night
Blown down his throat: stumbled through ruined hearths,
Proved all that muddy brown monotony
Where blood's the only coloured thing. Perhaps
Had seen a man killed, a sentry shot at night,
Hunched as he fell, his feet on the firing-step,

* stench.

His neck against the back slope of the trench,
And the rest doubled between, his head
Smashed like an eggshell and the warm grey brain
Spattered all bloody on the parados* . . .
Yet still God's in His Heaven, all is right
In this best possible of worlds . . .
God loves us, God looks down on this our strife
And smiles in pity, blows a pipe at times
And calls some warriors home . . .

How rare life is!
On earth, the love and fellowship of men,
Men sternly banded: banded for what end?
Banded to maim and kill their fellow men—
For even Huns are men. In Heaven above
A genial umpire, a good judge of sport
Won't let us hurt each other! Let's rejoice
God keeps us faithful, pens us still in fold.
Ah, what a faith is ours (almost, it seems,
Large as a mustard seed)—we trust and trust,
Nothing can shake us! Ah how good God is
To suffer us to be born just now, when youth
That else would rust, can slake his blade in gore
Whose very God Himself does seem to walk
The bloody fields of Flanders He so loves.

Night Patrol

ARTHUR GRAEME WEST

'Over the top! The wire's thin here, unbarbed
Plain rusty coils, not staked, and low enough:
Full of old tins, though—When you're through,
all three,

* back of trench, as opposed to 'parapet'.

Aim quarter left for fifty yards or so,
Then straight for that new piece of German wire;
See if it's thick, and listen for a while
For sounds of working; don't run any risks;
About an hour; now, over!'
                              And we placed
Our hands on the topmost sand-bags, leapt, and stood
A second with curved backs, then crept to the wire,
Wormed ourselves tinkling through, glanced back,
                              and dropped.
The sodden ground was splashed with shallow pools,
And tufts of crackling cornstalks, two years old,
No man had reaped, and patches of spring grass,
Half-seen, as rose and sank the flares, were strewn
With the wreck of our attack: the bandoliers,
Packs, rifles, bayonets, belts, and haversacks,
Shell fragments, and the huge whole forms of shells
Shot fruitlessly—and everywhere the dead.
Only the dead were always present—present
As a vile sickly smell of rottenness;
The rustling stubble and the early grass,
The slimy pools—the dead men stank through all,
Pungent and sharp; as bodies loomed before,
And as we passed, they stank; then dulled away
To that vague factor, all encompassing,
Infecting earth and air. They lay, all clothed,
Each in some new and piteous attitude
That we well marked to guide us back; as he,
Outside our wire, that lay on his back and crossed
His legs Crusader-wise; I smiled at that,
And thought of Elia* and his Temple Church.
From him, a quarter left, lay a small corpse,
Down in a hollow, huddled as in bed,
That one of us put his hand on unawares.

* Charles Lamb.

144

Next was a bunch of half a dozen men
All blown to bits, an archipelago
Of corrupt fragments, vexing to us three,
Who had no light to see by, save the flares.
On such a trail, so lit, for ninety yards
We crawled on belly and elbows, till we saw,
Instead of lumpish dead before our eyes,
The stakes and crosslines of the German wire.
We lay in shelter of the last dead man,
Ourselves as dead, and heard their shovels ring
Turning the earth, their talk and cough at times.
A sentry fired and a machine-gun spat;
They shot a flare above us, when it fell
And spluttered out in the pools of No Man's Land,
We turned and crawled past the remembered dead;
Past him and him, and them and him, until,
For he lay some way apart, we caught the scent
Of the Crusader and slid past his legs,
And through the wire and home, and got our rum.

3. After Marching

In Western Europe the marching ground to a halt. The French and Germans had each lost one and a half million men and Great Britain about a half that number, while Russian casualties have never been accurately assessed. On battlefronts further east there were still many more months before the fighting ended. The immediate postwar unrest felt in many European countries after the war was not acute in England. There was the characteristic muddle and delay in the process of demobilisation which made the general return 'up half-known roads' an anticlimax. Many of the demobilised had been ne'er-do-wells who quickly volunteered in 1914. The cheerful image of the English Tommy showed them all heroes while war lasted, but when they came home and were once more without jobs they were granted small sums of national assistance and rejected as layabouts. The cycle came round all too soon.

Writers of the 1920s seem to lack all joy and spontaneity: one would hardly think the greatest war in history (at that time) was over. If the physical rebuilding of Europe was swift, it only exposed a world full of newer and subtler forms of disorder and civil disturbance. To judge from the poems of Eliot and Pound the appropriate vision of postwar world was of commercial vulgarity and rampant philistinism. Eliot created a number of commercial grotesques such as Mr Burbank and Mr Bleistein, and in *The Waste Land* he seemed to admit no distinction between those who had died and those who had been drawn back into the postwar civilisation. His verdict on the period is: 'I had not thought death had undone so many.'

Ezra Pound, on the other hand, was ultimately more obsessed with the economic consequences of the peace and produced a stark account of the price of war in *Hugh Selwyn Mauberley*. Though it is not fair to either poet to quote lines as the precise expression of his own opinion—indeed they each take pains to hide behind a fictitious *persona*—the postwar disillusion is there at the end of Pound's lines about those who

> walked eye-deep in hell
> believing in old men's lies, then unbelieving
> came home, home to a lie,
> home to many deceits.

This is the view that Wilfred Owen would most probably have entertained if he had returned home, and it gives us reason for interpreting the years 1919 to 1939 as 'the long weekend' (to borrow another phrase from Robert Graves) during which another war was just around the corner.

Because prose is outside the scope of this collection novelists cannot receive adequate attention. Yet one realises that a book like *Howard's End* (1910) by E. M. Forster is a good deal more politically alert than any poetry of its day. The central characters are an intellectual family, the Schlegels, with whom the writer is identified. They fall behind and leave the commercially-minded Wilcoxes to possess England. In the end Forster writes of them: 'Logically they had no right to live'—not so much a prediction of a German war as a foretaste of the post-war period. Or again, there is Conrad's *Victory* finished early in 1914, in which the central character, Axel Heyst, tries to evade his fate by escaping to a remote island. Sent to the spot by a German, Schomberg, his enemies seek him out even there to imply the involvement of everyone in a total war.

Frederic Manning, Ford Madox Ford and Richard Aldington are three lesser novelists, represented in these pages by their poetry, who all wrote with penetration upon the pressures facing civilians and soldiers alike. To conclude this short list one must point to the Cornish 'Nightmare' scenes in D. H. Lawrence's *Kangaroo* of 1923 or his earlier *Women in Love* which seems the outstanding statement of the ideas of the period and the truest prose counterpart of Eliot's *The Waste Land*.

The Poems in this Section

Several poets have been referred to previously. These comments are on the writers who have not been introduced.

GILBERT FRANKAU was a fighter who revelled in the efficiency of the war mechanism: 'I am only a cog in a giant machine.'

Yet he is unable to accept that he had been gradually and permanently desensitised by the experience (p. 152). He pays the price suggested by his poem 'Poison'. Here is the effect of the atrocity story and the great lie pounded out by the propaganda machine. If such opinions were representative of 1918, then there could be no possibility of lasting international reconciliation or forgetting temporary differences. The two minutes' silence at the Cenotaph on Remembrance Day has much to answer for, with its theme of 'lest we forget'.

One sad figure has been present throughout this collection but has remained in the shadow. This is IVOR GURNEY, to whom one might apply Marvell's lines:

> What field of all the Civil Wars
> Where his were not the deepest Scars?

While fighting as a private soldier on the Somme he suffered from shellshock and afterwards was allowed to return to his musical studies in London. His two published volumes of poems are the work of a sensitive Georgian with the exceptional ability of writing both words and music. He is that now familiar figure, the Gloucestershire countryman in the middle of a war. What developed after his return to civilian life was a progressive mental decline, mitigated by periods of musical and literary creativity.

The special poignancy of Gurney's last years is that while confined in a mental home at Dartford in Kent he was always petitioning for his release. His requests took the form of a series of letters to church, police and other authorities, often accompanied by short poems. These despairing letters, in which he implored for death rather than the continuous crucifixion of the electric shock treatment in the asylum, make appalling reading. Together with an appeal to the Chief Inspector at a police station would go a slight but acceptable lyric, proof of schizophrenia. The fact that these letters and poems, though folded up for posting, were never sent and remain in the collection of his unpublished papers, poems and songs adds to the painful experience of looking through them.

Immediately before his death in 1937 Gurney was handed a copy of *Music Review* which contained several articles in his honour both as poet and composer. Recently it is as a composer of songs, challenging comparison with Peter Warlock, that

Ivor Gurney's name is best known. The collection of his manuscripts has had its vicissitudes, having been subject to temporary thefts and threatened piratical publication. For this reason especially, an authorised collection of his works is needed to place beside the posthumous selection made in 1954 by Edmund Blunden.

Here and there his poetic fragments show the influence of T. S. Eliot and Gerard Manley Hopkins as if one is reading the poetry of war experience written in a postwar idiom. Gurney unfortunately confused the past with the present, the Severn with the Somme, and imagined himself still on the battlefield years afterwards. Some of the poems, printed here for the first time, show a lack of polish but no deficiency in either observation or vocabulary. Their rhythms betray haphazardness and breathlessness but they are perhaps among the most moving documents. There is, to one's surprise, the echo of Brooke:

> When I am covered with the dust of peace
> And but this rain to moist my senseless clay,
> Will there be one regret left in that ill ease

as well as the imitation of Walt Whitman in 'Dirge for two Striplings' and 'Drum Taps'. At his delayed death Gurney was at one with all those anonymous, maimed and blinded ones addressed by Sassoon:

> Does it matter? Losing your sight? . . .
> There's such splendid work for the blind;
> And people will always be kind.

In a most lucid piece, 'War Books', he reaches a conclusion which can be compared with the later reflection on the subject by T. S. Eliot on p. 151. Gurney's opening which gives us a clear-headed retrospect, may be set down again as a pendant to his 'Poet before Battle' with which the collection of poetry opened and addressed to ourselves:

> What did they expect of our toil and extreme
> Hunger— the perfect drawing of a heart's dream?
> Did they look for a book of wrought art's perfection,
> Who promised no reading, nor praise, nor publica-
>   tion?
> Out of the heart's sickness the spirit wrote
> For delight, or to escape hunger, or of war's worst
>   anger.

The Veteran

EDMUND BLUNDEN

He stumbles silver-haired among his bees,
Now with the warm sun mantling him; he plods,
Taking his honey under the pippin-trees,
Where every sprig with rich red harvest nods.
    He marks the skies' intents,
And like a child, his joy still springing new,
In this fantastic garden the year through
He steeps himself in nature's opulence.

Mellow between the leafy maze smiles down
September's sun, swelling his multitude
Of gold and red and green and russet-brown
Lavished in plenty's lusty-handed mood
    For this old man who goes
Reckoning ripeness, shoring the lolling sprays,
And fruits which early gusts made castaways
From the deep grasses thriftily rescuing those.

Babble he will, lingeringly, lovingly,
Of all the glories of this fruitful place,
Counting the virtues of each several tree,
Her years, her yield, her hardihood or grace;
    While through this triumph-song,
As through their shielding leaves, the year's fruits burn
In bright eye-cozening colour, turn by turn,
From cool black cherries till gold quinces throng

Blossoming the blue mists with their queenly scent . . .
Who hearing him can think what dragging years
Of drouthy raids and frontier-fights he spent,

With drums and fife to drown his clamouring fears? . . .
   Here where the grapes turn red
On the red walls, and honey in the hives
Is like drift snow, contentment only thrives,
And the long misery of the Line is dead.

Resting in his old oaken-raftered room,
His sits and watches the departing light
Crimsoning like his apple-trees in bloom,
With dreaming gratitude and calm delight.
   And fast the peering sun
Has lit the blue delft ranged along the wall,
The painted clock and Squirrel's Funeral,
And through the cobwebs traced his rusty gun.

And then the dusk, and sleep, and while he sleeps,
Apple-scent floods and honey's fragrance there,
And old-time wines, whose secret he still keeps,
Are beautiful upon the marvelling air,
   And if sleep seem unsound,
And set old bugles pealing through the dark,
Waked on the instant, he but wakes to hark
His bellman cockerel crying the first round.

1919

A Note on War Poetry

T. S. ELIOT

Not the expression of collective emotion
Imperfectly reflected in the daily papers.
Where is the point at which the merely individual
Explosion breaks

In the path of an action merely typical
To create the universal, originate a symbol
Out of the impact? This is a meeting
On which we attend

Of forces beyond control by experiment—
Of Nature and the Spirit. Mostly the individual
Experience is too large, or too small. Our emotions
Are only 'incidents'

In the effort to keep day and night together.
It seems just possible that a poem might happen
To a very young man: but a poem is not poetry—
That is a life.

War is not a life: it is a situation,
One which may neither be ignored nor accepted,
A problem to be met with ambush and stratagem,
Enveloped or scattered.

The enduring is not a substitute for the transient,
Neither one for the other. But the abstract conception
Of private experience at its greatest intensity
Becoming universal, which we call 'poetry',
May be affirmed in verse.

1942

Poison

GILBERT FRANKAU

Forget, and forgive them—you say:
 War's bitterness passes;
Wild rose wreaths the gun-pit to-day,

Where the trench was, young grass is;
    Forget and forgive:
    Let them live.

Forgive them—you say—and forget;
    Since struggle is finished,
Shakes hands, be at peace, square the debt,
    Let old hates be diminished;
      Abandon blockade,
      Let them trade.

Fools! Shall the pard* change his skin
    Or cleanse one spot from it?
As the lecher returns to his sin
    So the cur to its vomit.
    Fools! Hath the Hun
    Earned place in the sun?

You who accuse that I fan
    War's spark from hate's ember,
Forgive and forget if you can;
    But, I, I remember
    Men who face death
    Choking for breath.

Four years back to a day—
    Men who fought cleanly.
Killed say you? Murdered, *I* say,
    Murdered, most meanly,
    Poisoned! . . . And yet,
    You can forget.

21 April 1919 (four years after the introduction of poison gas by the Germans at Ypres)

* leopard.

War Books

IVOR GURNEY

What did they expect of our toil and extreme
Hunger—the perfect drawing of a heart's dream?
Did they look for a book of wrought art's perfection,
Who promised no reading, nor praise, nor publication?
Out of the heart's sickness the spirit wrote
For delight, or to escape hunger, or of war's worst anger,
When the guns died to silence and men would gather sense
Somehow together, and find this was life indeed,
And praise another's nobleness, or to Cotswold get hence.
There we wrote—Corbie Ridge—or in Gonnehem at rest.
Or Fauquissart or world's death songs, ever the best.
One made sorrows' praise passing the Church where silence
Opened for the long quivering strokes of the bell—
Another wrote all soldiers' praise, and of France and hight's
    stars.
Served his guns, got immortality, and died well.
But Ypres played another trick with its danger on me,
Kept still the needing and loving of action body;
Gave no candles, and nearly killed me twice as well,
And no souvenirs though I risked my life in the stuck tanks,
Yet there was praise of Ypres, love came sweet in hospital
And old Flanders went under to long ages of plays thought
    in my pages.

Dirge for Two Striplings

IVOR GURNEY

God knows the eyes of one were steady and bright
A Company's delight—
And mine watching silent, the business of a poet.

The other of Gloucester born, that was, so men say, the
  one
God-like County of England—of all England.
He cursed his men and our men at Ypres and died,
Being sweet and tender-hearted and all-brave beside.
What tears by Blythe, what hurt by Severn there was
Is for the guess, but only our Gloucester Company's guess:
That had kindliness and sweetness of heart and grace,
For all their long marching, and endurance, Courage
  without praise,
Courtesy in billets, and nice manners in farms or
  estaminets,
The Severn Valley goodness coming out in courteous
  ways.
And as for the North—the miners with small food kept
Would make a feed for soldiers while their hunger slept,
With bright flame, which all-giving generousness and a
  recklessness of living
As in dying one had—with no blot on them, and good-
  ness to amaze.

Ypres

IVOR GURNEY

North French air may make any flat land clear and beautiful,
But East of Ypres scarred was most foul and dreadful
With stuck tanks, ruined bodies needing quick honour's burial,
But yet sunset, first morning, hallowed all, awed, made mys-
  terious
The ugly lives of land running to eastward; the Front of us,
Worse things of conflict not yet hidden unseen underground.
(Shall we also fall stricken by one steel shard, sicken

The air with stenches, that were of Gloucestershire villages,
Be buried with haste, horror; by those were comrades before,
Lie, clovered, rot, with no hope but to make meadows quicken
When Time has cleared this dreadful earth of infinite brute
      carnages;
And left some clean stuff; earth, beautiful—as once bodies
      were?)
But the place was most hideous at times, of mankind all
      unheedful;
And we forgot all battle-honours—all glories storial,
Our country's birth, (our great pride) that would make stir us
Even on the brink of the grave to the risk of warfare.
Only the half light's wonder gave us remind (made heart kind)
Of the villages and dear households we had left foolish and
      all-dutiful—
(But too rashly for such vile pain, and gray hideousness)
At Ypres—the talk of soldiers was the one delight there,
The one goodness, greatness of bearing Hell-from-high without
      fear.

Picture of Two Veterans

IVOR GURNEY

We liked you, but you got frost-feet, went down too soon:
You took the lightest bags, and did fatigue, leaving alone
Line Service—with a trust in Providence heavy on your
      platoon.
Well, you had your way, and Grandcourt finished your
      service.
(You would have held and died, but your place was with
      your families).
Yours was no frame for Vermand or dreadful-earth Ypres,
You passed down trench—and got to the Dressing Station;

We granted you right (and envy) to your right elation,
Who stayed and expected parcels from a grateful nation,
But got few, Base pinched some, and sly Transport for
   candles,
They got to us ragged, with neither string straight nor
   handles,
And you had plenty in Blighty, and bread in bundles.

When I am Covered

IVOR GURNEY

When I am covered with the dust of peace
And but this rain to moist my senseless clay,
Will there be one regret left in that ill ease

One sentimental fit of light and day—
A grief for hillside and the beaten trees?
Better to leave them utterly to go away.
When every tiny pang of love is counterpiece
To shadowed woe of huge weight and the stay
For yet another torment ere release

Better to lie and be forgotten aye:
In Death his role leaves never a creane.
Rest squares reckonings Love set awry.

from 'Hugh Selwyn Mauberley'

EZRA POUND

These fought in any case,
and some believing,
          pro domo, in any case . . .

Some quick to arm,
some for adventure,
some from fear of weakness,
some from fear of censure,
some for love of slaughter, in imagination,
learning later . . .
some in fear, learning love of slaughter;

Died some, pro patria,
              non 'dulce' non 'et decor' . . .
walked eye-deep in hell
believing in old men's lies, then unbelieving
came home, home to a lie,
home to many deceits,
home to old lies and new infamy;
usury age-old and age-thick
and liars in public places.

Daring as never before, wastage as never before.
Young blood and high blood,
fair cheeks, and fine bodies;

fortitude as never before,

frankness as never before,
disillusions as never told in the old days,
hysterias, trench confessions,
laughter out of dead bellies.

Aftermath

SIEGFRIED SASSOON

Have you forgotten yet? . . .
For the world's events have rumbled on since those gagged
    days,

Like traffic checked while at the crossing of city-ways:
And the haunted gap in your mind has filled with thoughts that
    flow
Like clouds in the lit heaven of life; and you're a man reprieved
    to go,
Taking your peaceful share of Time, with joy to spare.
But the past is just the same—and War's a bloody game . . .
Have you forgotten yet? . . .
Look down, and swear by the slain of the War that you'll never forget.

Do you remember the dark months you held the sector at
    Mametz—
The nights you watched and wired and dug and piled sandbags
    on parapets?
Do you remember the rats; and the stench
Of corpses rotting in front of the front-line trench—
And dawn coming, dirty-white, and chill with the hopeless
    rain?
Do you ever stop and ask, 'Is it all going to happen again?'

Do you remember that hour of din before the attack—
And the anger, the blind compassion that seized and shook you
    then
As you peered at the doomed and haggard faces of your men?
Do you remember the stretcher-cases lurching back
With dying eyes and lolling heads—those ashen-grey
Masks of the lads who once were keen and kind and gay?

Have you forgotten yet? . . .
Look up, and swear by the green of the spring that you'll never forget.

March 1919

Afterword

It has always been a popular question: what happened to poetry in World War II? One can brush it aside by explaining that nobody of sufficient talent emerged at that time, but it is undeniable that a number of poems was written even if unknown to a large public. Sidney Keyes, Alun Lewis and Keith Douglas are three writers who were killed by the enemy yet failed to establish themselves as the Owens or Rosenbergs of their generation. Several older men out of World War I were still writing and two recent anthologies have been published to declare that poetry did not dry up.

From the start there was probably less idealism when conscription was immediately introduced. Many men of superior education—the potential poets—were drafted into strategic, educational, intelligence and even civil service work instead of being sent to the front. This had the joint effects of preserving their lives and shielding them from exactly the experiences of battle that once roused their less sheltered predecessors to poetry.

Since the purpose of most earlier war poetry had been urgent communication and warning, this was less necessary in 1939 when there was abundant information from press and radio. Furthermore, it was as dangerous to live in London or Coventry as to be 'somewhere in France', so that the terrors of war were no longer distant or obscure. No civilian poet in 1940 or 1941 would emulate the pathetically comic little piece by Herbert Palmer on p. 102:

> I never feel more cheerfulness
> Than when the German raiders fly
> Like bees across the cloudless sky.

On the nights of fire-bombs and high explosives over England it was difficult to remain cheerful. Although there exist paintings by Henry Moore of Londoners in air-raid shelters in the Tube stations, there is no equally striking poetry to catch the same documentary impression.

Three poems by established writers were, however, born out of the attacks by fire-bombs: the fire section of *Little Gidding* by T. S. Eliot, 'Refusal to mourn' by Dylan Thomas, and 'Still Falls the Rain' by Edith Sitwell. Outstanding among sophisticated poems are those by Henry Reed, some of them only quite recently completed, and 'Soldiers Bathing', by F. T. Prince, which reminds us a little of Rosenberg.

What was decisively lacking was a true public for new verse. The most admired writers in 1939, W. H. Auden, C. Day Lewis and Louis MacNeice were too far towards the political left to strike attitudes nationally respectable and representative, and they and others were inclined to withdraw from public themes. A final minor practical point should be noted. In the economics of book publishing the years 1940 to 1945 were highly unpromising through stringent war economy paper-rationing measures, so that only the most established writers could expect to remain in print. Where in the First War there were some 500 small volumes of new verse, it is doubtful whether in the Second there were as many as ten per cent of that number.

Was there—it may seem to us—any point in continuing to write about rifles, tanks and dug-outs with only a slightly newer slant? In the poems in this anthology of Jeffery Day and Paul Bewsher there are already voices from the air and at the same time the French poet Apollinaire had imagined supernatural glints in the searchlights. Much of this in 1939 was bound to be old wine in new bottles. Looking back now for the great symbols of the Second War we are forced upon the bombing of Hiroshima and the slaughter of millions in the Nazi death camps, events in which the British had no hand.

The war which opened in September 1939 with an attack upon Poland had as one of its final acts the liberation, from Oswiecim in Poland, of those that remained alive in the concentration camp of Auschwitz there. Today we can travel to see it just as from 1919 it was possible to tour the battlefields. Now the visitor finds a hill of human hair, a mound of cases and small personal possessions, the gas chambers and the incinerators. There is a great deal which is overpowering as a stimulus to the imagination and a challenge to the human conscience. Most piercing of all are the rows and rows of photographs of men and women all with shaven heads who stare down and haunt the viewer.

It is not surprising that a visitor's school of poetry has emerged from expeditions to Auschwitz and Belsen. Three poems that may be mentioned are 'Annotations of Auschwitz' by Peter Porter, 'Daddy' by Sylvia Plath, and 'Report to the Director' by George MacBeth. At the moment, these poems may appear sensational, reduced to the level of such manifestations of literary violence as the poems of Thom Gunn and Ted Hughes, the plays of Harold Pinter or the novels of James Baldwin.

World War I has not yet lost its power over contemporary writers either. Inevitably each Remembrance Day offers a moment to think of the dead of both wars and to summon up visions of each. Vernon Scannell is a contemporary poet who has devoted a couple of poems to the war that he did not know. In his 'Remembrance Day' he sees the subject not critically, but almost without emotion:

> But wormy years have eaten their
> Identities and none can mourn
> These artificial dead.

To conclude we should perhaps notice the relevance of the great strain of cruelty that inhabits much of our literature. Shakespeare, after all, gave us *Titus Andronicus* and the horrific scenes in *King Lear*. The Gothic horror novels written at the end of the eighteenth century (such as *The Monk* by M. G. Lewis) had a very large following. A later example in this genre is Mary Shelley's *Frankenstein*, a book rich in psychological revelation of its writer and of the public at which she aimed it. In our own century, Kipling and Henley have been mentioned already. Immediately before the outbreak of the war in 1914 there was a growing movement among intellectual anarchists to worship the concept of speed and cruelty. This owed its inspiration to the Italian Futurist Marinetti and the sculptor Gaudier-Brzeska, who was a close friend of Ezra Pound. In many of the *avant-garde* movements immediately before 1914, as Bernard Bergonzi points out in his *Heroes' Twilight*, there was an intimate relation between the excitement of physical force and the sensation of artistic creation. Any satisfied reader of *avant-garde* manifestoes would have drawn considerable pleasure also from the poetry of the later years of the war. To immerse oneself in a poem on being run over by a tank or sinking into the mud is to fall into an ambiguous state. One may rationalise the process as an effort to discover the insane horror of war with the aim of demonstrating against it, but one will also know that deep disturbance in which the mind assents to the scene and would like to encourage it afresh. Dwelling too long on the mental state of the man who inflicts a wound on himself in order to be sent out of the front line, or on the terror of a deserter may arouse in the reader a series of fantasies which do him harm. It is that process of enjoying what is degrading which is given the German name *schadenfreude*, a form of getting things both ways. The modern understanding of human psychology enables us to see the lust for power and cruelty as something basic in human personality. No reading will ever correct it and poetry is not a substitute for morality or theology. It is the same latent aggressiveness that leads mankind to find new and more efficient methods of destruction in all our technological advances. There is no need to diagnose the violence in the modern mass media of communication here, since complaints against it are so frequent, but it is within such an overall atmosphere—highly sophisticated and self-aware—that many readers turn once more to the study of war literature.

A great degree of reader-involvement is demanded by war poetry, though it was intended by the artist to point in the direction of tragedy, humanity or pacifism. When the writer has done his job well, avoids both hypocrisy in his attitudes and naiveté in his style, such discussion can be made critically relevant to our own day. The desire for a scrupulous attention to the moral, political and psychological problems of warfare in few words makes war poetry so fine a focus for discussion, and this is far more important a motive for reading it than a factitious modern excuse such as 'We're living under the shadow of the Bomb'. There can be no more compelling and immediate way of turning from twentieth-century poetry to the discussion of our own artistic and philosophical problems than in selecting from among the varied examples provided in this anthology. The compression of the slightest piece of lyric verse written on public and private themes endures a vast expansion if it starts with the subject-matter of war experiences gained between 1914 and 1918, when—in Wilfred Owen's terms—both the poetry and the pity existed side by side.

Biographical Notes

RICHARD ALDINGTON
(1892–1962)

First came into prominence as a member of the Imagist Group and married the American Hilda Doolittle, another member of it. His active war service took place between 1916 and 1918. During that time he wrote a number of Imagist poems upon warfare and was one of the few to do so. His poems were collected in 1929, the year which saw the publication of his long-meditated antiwar novel *Death of a Hero*. In later years he edited and translated a considerable amount of literature and became a figure of controversy with his biographies of D. H. Lawrence (*Portrait of a Genius, But...*) and T. E. Lawrence (*Lawrence of Arabia, a Biographical Enquiry*). A further collection of his poems appeared in 1948. Uncollected poems with a critical evaluation appeared in 1974 (Rider College Publications, U.S.A.).

ALFRED AUSTIN
(1835–1913)

His early poetry was satirical but he made his reputation as the voice of the Tory government of Lord Salisbury in the 1890s. In 1895 he celebrated the Jameson Raid which led to the outbreak of the Boer War and earned the Poet Laureateship with his poetic support of the imperialist cause. He wrote his *Autobiography* in 1911, but his large body of poetry has not been collected and is very little read at the present.

MACKENZIE BELL
(1856–1930)

A poet, critic and traveller who gave lectures on the conduct of the war with lantern slides. His *Poetical Pictures of the Great War* was a series of poems written for these occasions, and the curiosity reprinted here is from his 1917 vintage. He published his *Selected Poems* in 1921, and a biography entitled *The Balance of Life* by A. Egerton Smythe appeared as recently as 1955.

PAUL BEWSHER
(1894–1966)

One of the first writers to take the theme of aerial warfare. After the war he devoted himself mainly to journalism.

LAURENCE BINYON
(1869–1943)

Most of his writings are devoted to the study of oriental art upon which he was an expert. His war service was confined to a period as a hospital orderly in 1916. Throughout the war, however, he became adept at composing poetry in the 'official' manner. His 'For the Fallen', though written early, is associated with the commemoration of the casualties of the war at the Cenotaph afterwards. His books *The Four Years* (1919) and *Collected Poems* (1931) contain all these writings.

EDMUND BLUNDEN
(1896–1974)

For long associated with Oxford University. After the war he held his war poems back and made his reputation with pastoral pieces. With his distinguished prose work *Undertones of War* (1929) he completed his literary record of war experience. For many years he was a professor of English literature in the universities of Tokyo and Hong Kong. He now lives in Suffolk and was Professor of Poetry at Oxford in the mid-sixties. His *Poems of Many Years* (1957) provides a representative collection; a booklet about him and his work has been written by A. M. Hardie for the British Council. He is represented in Sydney Bolt's *Poetry of the 1920s*.

RUPERT BROOKE
(1887–1915)

His reputation as a figure of legend should not obscure the fact that he was a promising Elizabethan scholar and one of the founders of the celebrated Marlowe Society of Cambridge University, which has since become an accepted standard for the performance of classical plays. He was also well known in university circles as a Fabian socialist. He published his first book of poetry in 1911. It was the appearance of his war poems, *1914*, and his romantic death in the Aegean that made him into a national hero. His poems were finally collected in 1946 by his friend Geoffrey Keynes, and in 1963 there appeared a long biography (still, however, an incomplete one) by Christopher Hassall, which is a good guide to the literary, political and academic circles in which many war writers lived.

LESLIE COULSON
(1889–1916)
A journalist before the outbreak of war, he was one of the very few writers to establish a reputation as a poet from the ranks: almost all the other poets became officers. His complete poetic output appeared after his death in *From an Outpost* (1917).

JEFFERY DAY
(1896–1918)
A celebrated air ace in his day, he was killed when he was shot down. Like the poems of Bewsher, those of Day are especially interesting as the first examples of a form of experience that was then completely novel. It may be agreed that he succeeded in showing the unexpected attraction of his subject.

T. S. ELIOT
(1888–1965)
Anglo-American poet, dramatist and critic who was educated at Harvard College and the Sorbonne, Paris. His importance as a poet and intellectual during the present century has been extremely high. Although *Prufrock* (dedicated to a fallen soldier) and other early poems appeared in 1917, they are unrelated to the general experience of the period. Not until after the war and the publication of *The Waste Land* in 1922 did he fully present the mood of postwar Europe and made himself a spokesman (albeit unwillingly) of his generation. Writing for American readers at the time he compared the critical mood of the 1920s on either side of the Atlantic, yet as time passed he became more closely identified with the English side of it. His career as a dramatist began with his highly successful verse play *Murder in the Cathedral* (1935), and the finest of his late poems, the cycle *Four Quartets* (completed in 1943), finds space for images derived from the raids upon London in World War II. It was a request received during the Second War that elicited the poem on p. 151, which is included as a characteristically phrased comment upon the writers of both wars. He himself had not recorded such experiences out of a feeling that the

writer is obliged to distance himself from anything which would prove too disturbing.

W. N. EWER
(1885–1977)
His main publications were in the field of foreign diplomacy and relations. His poem 'Five Souls' was popular and became the inspiration of a pageant in the 1930s.

FORD MADOX FORD
(1873–1939)
A voluminous writer in every field. He was born Ford Madox Hueffer and wrote under this name until the 1920s. His collaboration with Joseph Conrad has been much discussed and several writers including Ezra Pound and Ernest Hemingway have expressed their indebtedness to him. He joined up, it is said, to escape from the greater warfare of his stormy domestic life and after the war he devoted himself more to the publication of novels which have attracted increasing attention in recent years. The chief of these is the tetralogy known as *Parade's End* which appeared in four separate books between 1924 and 1928. His poetry was collected in 1936. A pamphlet by Kenneth Young provides a long bibliography.

GILBERT FRANKAU
(1884–1952)
His main work was in the form of the popular novel, but he fought throughout the war and collected his poetry together in 1923.

JOHN FREEMAN
(1880–1929)
A poet who split his life between business and poetry. His wartime productions are of the patriotic order and his authentic voice is to be found in his escapist countryside pieces, collected in 1928.

ROBERT FROST
(1878–1962)
Although he was a Californian he deserves a place in a volume mainly devoted to English writing because he settled in

Gloucestershire between 1912 and 1915 and was well known to many English writers living in the neighbourhood, chief among whom was Edward Thomas. His first publication took place in England in 1913, but on his return to America he established himself for decades as an admired and original poetic voice. His work, like that of Hardy, has been widely praised for its handling of colloquial language. In 1955 a convenient selection was published in England by Penguin Books. Elizabeth Jennings's study, *Robert Frost* (1964) contains an introduction to his large output.

WILFRID WILSON GIBSON
(1878–1962)

Born in Northumberland and confronted there with the problems of industrial life. He was not of suitable physique for military service although he spent a short time in the ranks, drawing upon his experiences for his best war poems. His later war poetry lacks the distinctive note of savageness we find in the poems in the volume *Battle* (1916). After the war he lived in Gloucestershire within easy reach of the influential poet, Lascelles Abercrombie. He had been a close friend of Rupert Brooke, and as one of his legatees he was assured of a large income. He won the Hawthornden Prize in 1920 and his *Collected Poems* of 1926 gives an indication of his fluency as a writer.

ROBERT GRAVES
(1895–   )

A Georgian poet who has continued writing and earning a continuously fresh reputation all the time. Most unusually he has removed most of his early work (including his war poems) from circulation. A friend of both Sassoon and Owen, he was, like them, deeply involved in active service. He described his experiences fully in his autobiography *Goodbye to All That*, which appeared in 1929. He then went to live in Majorca where he has remained, publishing novels, poems and works upon mythology. He was Professor of Poetry at Oxford (1961–66) and on the occasion of his seventieth birthday declared that he would go on strike, having been for too long a one-man literary factory. All that he writes is of wide interest and much of it is extremely controversial. A study of his work by J. M. Cohen gives an introduction to his learning and sensibility.

JULIAN GRENFELL
(1888–1915)

An Old Etonian who was a member of the Regular Army before the war. He retained his ideals and beliefs in the traditions of the Army until his death. He wrote little apart from one masterpiece which is often considered superior to the poems of Rupert Brooke in similar vein. His brother William was also a writer, and the poem by Robert Nichols on p. 94 is dedicated to him. In 1917 a short memoir of Julian was written by Viola Meynell.

IVOR GURNEY
(1890–1937)

Gifted in both music and literature, he is extremely well represented in the present collection. He studied music both in Gloucester, where he was born, and in London at the Royal College of Music. After service in the ranks he was withdrawn from the Somme with shellshock and returned to musical studies. However, his personality was unbalanced by the war and he was confined at different times in mental homes, still composing both music and poetry there. His poetry was published in collections in 1917 and 1919 and again, posthumously, in 1954. Several of his songs have been published and a number of them recorded for the gramophone. In his last years he was unable to distinguish the present and the past so that he continued to write what may be classified as 'war poems' for many years. A collection of his poems appeared in 1973.

THOMAS HARDY
(1840–1928)

Originally trained as an architect, he developed into one of the major writers of his period, first as a novelist and then as a poet. His large collection of poems is now accepted as a major element in the formation of modern poetic style. He influenced Sassoon and Graves and was a natural leader of the Georgian writers who shared his experience of the countryside but not his sharp eye and ironic tone. Among many books devoted to his work we may single out that by Douglas Brown, published in 1954 and *A Preface to Hardy* by Merryn Williams (1976).

F. W. HARVEY
(1888–1957)

A member of the Gloucestershire school of poets, in later life he made it a rule never to sleep for a single night outside his native county. During the war he was imprisoned in the camp at Gütersloh; while there he described prison-camp life and recalled his earlier surroundings. After his war poems, which were posted out of the camp and published in 1917 and 1919, he continued to write with a Georgian bias and practised as a solicitor until his death.

W. E. HENLEY
(1849–1903)

An influential critic and editor, dramatist and poet. Born in Gloucester he suffered a long spell in hospital. His best poems describe hospital life and London scenes, though his 'Song of the Sword' (another poem in praise of violence) and 'Invictus' are probably his most familiar compositions. He was a close friend and collaborator of Robert Louis Stevenson and with his handling of *vers-libre* was thought to be a potent influence upon young writers' experiments in prosody. The most recent treatment of his career is to be found in John Connell's *W. E. Henley* (1949).

WILLIAM NOEL HODGSON
(1893–1916)

While still at Oxford and under the influence of Rupert Brooke, he volunteered for army service. His poems, especially the prophetic one on p. 78, were extremely popular when they appeared in his posthumous collection *Verse and Prose in Peace and War* (1916).

LAURENCE HOUSMAN
(1865–1959)

Brother of A. E. Housman, trained as an artist and an art critic. His literary reputation was ensured with his plays upon St Francis, St Clare and Queen Victoria during the 1920s and

1930s. His poetry was collected in 1937. He also edited *War Letters of fallen Englishmen* (1930).

DYNELEY HUSSEY
(1893–1972)
After an education at Oxford and a period in the Army he developed an unusual combination of professions: music critic and Admiralty official. Only one volume of poetry, *Fleur de Lys* (1919) stands to his credit, his widest acclaim coming from his books upon Mozart and Verdi.

JAMES JOYCE
(1882–1941)
One of the most influential of all *avant-garde* writers in Europe. After leaving Dublin he settled on the continent. During World War I he was for a time in Switzerland, where he wrote the poem on p. 82, a typically spirited and comic attack by an Irishman upon the English bureaucracy in a neutral country. His work includes few poems. His semi-autobiographical fantasy novels *Ulysses* and *Finnegans Wake* remain his monuments. Richard Ellmann's long biography is the source of this poem and several other short pieces not published separately.

RUDYARD KIPLING
(1865–1936)
A journalist, novelist and poet, who was born in Bombay and achieved fame with his Indian tales. Awarded the Nobel Prize in 1907, he was already popular as the creator of stories with an imperialist bias, a whole mythology, and a mine of quotations which show no sign of losing ground. The poems represented in the anthology show him questioning and denying some of his earlier attitudes as the result of losing his only son in the war. The definitive edition of his poetry appeared in 1940. Recent studies of his output include those by C. E. Carrington and J. M. S. Tompkins.

D. H. LAWRENCE
(1885–1930)
The son of a Nottinghamshire coalminer, he became a clerk and a teacher before devoting himself to writing. Since his death he has been recognised as the most important and imaginative of

novelists from his generation. *Sons and Lovers*, his early novel, is a fictional account of his life: for a complete account of his career see Harry T. Moore, *Life and Works of D. H. Lawrence* (1963). His reputation as a critic also stands high at the present time and his poetry, which shows his development as both a Georgian and an Imagist, is collected in two large volumes published in 1964. For a short survey the reader is directed to Anthony Beal's *D. H. Lawrence* (1961).

FRANCIS LEDWIDGE
(1891–1917)
An Irish pauper with a naïve Celtic vision, an unusual innocence of outlook and an undisciplined technique. He was sponsored as a poet by Lord Dunsany and published three volumes of verse which were collected in 1955.

FREDERIC MANNING
(*c.* 1880–1935)
An Australian educated in England who published a number of poems before the war, together with essays and imaginary conversations. His wartime experience in the Shropshire Light Infantry provided the substance for his later poems and his novel, *Her Privates We*, published under the guise of 'Private 19022'. Reclusive, frail and asthmatic, he was termed 'an intellectual of intellectuals', a fact which allows us to judge the cost to him of being in a position to write this important novel which appeared in an unexpurgated text as recently as 1964.

ALICE MEYNELL
(1850–1922)
As a girl she lived in Italy writing poetry from an early age as Alice Thompson. Her poetry was collected in 1923 and has been occasionally reprinted.

HAROLD MONRO
(1879–1932)
Born in Brussels, he became famous more for his editorial work than for his own poetry. In 1913 he founded the Poetry Bookshop which became one of the platforms for writers and a sign of the acceleration of interest in poetry that occurred both in America and European countries before 1914. He fought on

anti-aircraft operations. His poetry was collected in 1933. For a further selection of his more characteristic work and for an appraisal of him, see Sydney Bolt, *English Poetry in the Twenties*, a companion volume in this series.

E. A. MACKINTOSH
(1893–1917)

An officer in a Highland Regiment who was wounded in action, he returned home for convalescence and met his death at his second encounter with the fighting. His books were *Highland Regiment* (1917) and *War the Liberator* (1918).

HENRY NEWBOLT
(1862–1939)

Educated at Clifton College (the background of several of his poems) and at Oxford. He is most familiar for his patriotic verses and those with a nautical flavour. These won him both a wide public and a knighthood in 1915. He spent many years in legal practice before making literature, criticism and the documentation of naval history his main pursuits. His poetry appeared in collections in 1912 and 1919 and for biography there is *The Later Life of Sir Henry Newbolt* (1942) by M. Newbolt.

ROBERT NICHOLS
(1893–1944)

Between 1914 and 1916 he was on active service and wrote poems that were published between 1915 and 1917. After that time he was sent to the U.S.A. as an official lecturer on behalf of the British Government. There he gave many readings (said to have been highly emotional) of his own poetry and that of his more famous contemporaries. The colloquial, onomatopoeic style of many of his poems at one time seemed modern and daring; possibly for this reason they have been extremely well represented in many anthologies. Now they seem contrived. He took over the Chair of English at Tokyo University after the war and continued to write poetry. A conspectus of his work is to be found in the volume *Such was My Singing* (1942). In the following year he edited a compilation of the verse of World War I, remarkable for the extreme length of the dialogue that forms the introduction.

EVERARD OWEN
(1860–1949)
A classics master at Harrow, a clergyman and also a Fellow of New College, Oxford. His poem 'Three Hills' is a simple and popular example of the public school war poem.

WILFRED OWEN
(1893–1918)
For most modern readers he is the poetic hero of World War I, who has achieved a reputation that continues to grow. When he was twenty he went to France as a private tutor and while there was introduced to the work of such French poets as Laurent Teilhade. Though he matriculated for London University he did not study there, and living in the Midlands he was out of touch with the literary culture of London before the War. He joined the Army in 1915 and was invalided home to Craiglockhart Hospital near Edinburgh, where he met Sassoon whose work he had already studied. He returned to the battlefield in the summer of 1918 having found a still deeper intensity in his writing and was killed a week before the Armistice. Not until the outbreak of World War II did he have a wide public and this has gained most recent impetus through the incorporation of nine of his poems in Benjamin Britten's *War Requiem*. In 1960 there came D. S. R. Welland's study of the poetry, and Harold Owen has written a distinguished three-volume biography of his brother under the title *Journey to Obscurity*. J. Stallworthy's *Wilfred Owen* (1974) is now the major biography.

HERBERT PALMER
(1880–1961)
Educated in England and Germany, he was a teacher until he retired in 1921 to devote his time to literature. He was a critic and satirist of the work of T. S. Eliot, publishing a poem entitled *Cinder Thursday* as a parody of Eliot's *Ash Wednesday*. His *Collected Poems* of 1933 was followed by several other volumes. The poem on p. 102 has a curiosity value in the light of the air raids in World War II.

EDEN PHILLPOTTS
(1862–1960)

Like Kipling, he was born in India. He settled in England first
as an insurance clerk and later as a novelist and playwright.
Most of his literary output is popular in tone and West Country
in outlook, arising from observation of life in Devonshire
where he lived. A tribute to him was published on his nine-
tieth birthday from which information may be obtained. His
war poetry was published in 1917 under the title *Plain Song*.

MAX PLOWMAN
(1883–1941)

Distinguished as a critic and as the editor of the quarterly, *The
Adelphi*, he was a prominent member of antiwar movements.
In addition to a number of war poems he published a prose
book entitled *A Subaltern on the Somme* in 1927, based on his
experiences.

EZRA POUND
(1885–1972)

An American from Idaho who specialised in the study and
translation of Romance and Oriental languages and settled in
Europe from 1908. His life in England brought him into contact with a number of the most prominent of *avant-garde* artists,
such as T. S. Eliot, James Joyce, Percy Wyndham Lewis and
Henri Gaudier-Brzeska, the sculptor. He was associated with
the formation of the Imagist movement and published poetry
regularly after 1908. *Hugh Selwyn Mauberley* (1920) was being
written during the War as a commentary upon life and culture
in England at the time. His long poem *Cantos* has been in
composition since the postwar years and published in instal-
ments. His *Selected Poems* (with an introduction by T. S. Eliot)
appeared first in 1928 and a booklet on his work by G. S.
Fraser (1960) provides necessary information.

HERBERT READ
(1893–1968)

A farmer's son who has lived for many years in Yorkshire and
has been identified with many aesthetic and political movements. His war verse came under the influence of the Imagists
and after the war he became one of the most distinguished of

art critics, preoccupied with the state of industrial design as well as the fine arts. He has written a quantity of literary criticism, especially upon Romantic and modern poets. The latest edition of his *Collected Poems* was published in 1966. A long poem entitled 'End of a War' was published several years after the Armistice, and in 1940 he returned to the theme of war poetry with a poem 'To a Conscript of 1940'. His autobiography, entitled *The Innocent Eye*, came out in 1947 and a booklet on his writings, by Francis Berry, in 1953.

EDGELL RICKWORD
(1898–   )
A distinguished but neglected poet whose style was formed in the 1920s. He became a prominent critic and edited *The Calendar of Modern Letters* from 1925–7 which was reprinted in its entirety in 1966. His *Collected Poems* of 1947 is a guide to the literary taste of thirty years and contains excellent work. More of his poetry appears in the companion collection, *Poetry of the 1920s*.

ISAAC ROSENBERG
(1890–1918)
Born in Bristol, he lived in Stepney and studied art before moving to South Africa where he was at the outbreak of war. His prewar poetry was in the Romantic vein transformed gradually by a study of the technique of Imagism. The war poems show him to have achieved an intensity of vision comparable with that of Blake. Physically he was poorly adapted to soldiering and he was unable to rise in the ranks, a circumstance that made life for him still harder. Hardship and inconvenience seem not to have impeded his vision, and his poetry has in some quarters been found preferable to Owen's. Collected editions of his works appeared in 1935 and 1949, and one of his editors, D. W. Harding, has an important essay on Rosenberg and the art of poetry in his book *Experience into Words*. Two biographies, one by J. Cohen and the other by J. Liddiard, appeared in 1975.

SIEGFRIED SASSOON
(1886–1967)
Probably the most distinguished of the trench poets to have survived two wars. Although he was born to the life of the rich

country gentleman he threw himself bravely and whole-heartedly into the fighting. His early poetry is of a Georgian order but he was swiftly converted into a horrified satirist by the vision of waste and terror that assailed soldiers on the Western Front. He narrowly risked court-martial as a pacifist and became the mentor of Wilfred Owen whom he met in the Craiglockhart Hospital near Edinburgh. His postwar poetry retained the same satirical note and returned to the themes and places associated with the war. He wrote his autobiography after the war and in *Memoirs of an Infantry Officer* (1930) described his experiences in the trenches. In recent years he has written less, his *Collected Poems* being published in 1961. A study of his work by Michael Thorpe appeared in 1966.

OSBERT SITWELL
(1892–1969)

An Old Etonian and Grenadier Guard with experience of the military life in peacetime. His book *Great Morning* exposed the unpreparedness of the professional soldier before 1914. His war service brought him into acquaintance with Sassoon and Owen, who increased his mood of satirical bitterness. After the war he was associated with his brother Sacheverell and his sister Edith in a number of literary ventures. Where they set out to scare and irritate they ended by being figures of power and prominence in the literary world out of proportion with the value of their own work. Sir Osbert's poetry was published in 1919, 1931 and 1943, while his most popular writings have been his volumes of autobiography, *Left Hand, Right Hand* (5 vols., 1945–50).

CHARLES HAMILTON SORLEY
(1895–1915)

A member of an academic family who enlisted in 1914 after spending a summer in Germany instead of taking up a place at Oxford University. His published verse shows a swiftly-maturing personality which possessed the highest potential greatness. His small book, *Marlborough and other Poems*, has often been admired and proved the source for the deepest of regrets. A recent study of his brief life is to be found in *The Ungirt Runner* (1965) by Burnett Swann.

(1897–1916)

He joined the Grenadiers at the age of seventeen and served alongside Osbert Sitwell. His death on the Somme allowed him very little time to write. A short memoir of him by his mother, Pamela, Lady Glenconner, is the source of our information about him.

EDWARD THOMAS
(1878–1917)

Already established as a writer of travel and descriptive prose before the war under the pseudonym of Edward Eastaway, he turned to poetry at the suggestion of Robert Frost, who settled in his neighbourhood. Most of his poetry conveys rustic scenery with subtlety and integrity of imagination. His widow. Helen Thomas, wrote an account of his early days and Eleanor Farjeon in *The Last Four Years* (1958) has a more significant theme and includes some study of his manuscripts. The first collected volume of his poetry appeared in 1922, since when it has been widely read. The first complete critical biography is that by William Cooke (1970), while a study of his writings by H. Coombes (1956) should also be consulted.

HERBERT TRENCH
(1865–1923)

An Irishman who worked for the Board of Education and lived for a time in Italy. He wrote a number of poems and plays, and after his death they were collected in three volumes in 1924.

WALTER JAMES TURNER
(1889–1946)

Born and educated in Melbourne, he was noted as a literary, dramatic and, above all, music critic, and author of several books on music, notably a study of Berlioz. From 1916 onwards he published volumes of poetry. His *Selected Poems* of 1939 show his development as a poet. The poem in the present anthology was written during his period of service in the Royal Garrison Artillery. At the end of his life he was Literary Editor of *The Spectator*. His work also appears in S. Bolt's *Poetry of the 1920s*, in this series.

(1875–1917)
Of French descent, he had already a few novels before the war;
then, although he was twice the age of many of the young poets,
he enlisted with all their idealism. 'No man could look more
lazy and no man was more active', was the verdict expressed by
G. K. Chesterton, an old school friend. His *War Poems* were
published after his death in 1918.

WILLIAM WATSON
(1858–1935)
A forgotten poet who was accepted as an official voice during
the Edwardian period and, more notably, during the early
stages of the War. In this he reversed the position he had
adopted during the Boer War. History has shown that few
writers have remained consistently critical of war during their
careers. Watson published collected volumes of his poetry in
1906 and 1928 and earned a knighthood for his propaganda
poetry in 1917.

ARTHUR GRAEME WEST
(1891–1917)
Born in Norwich and educated at Oxford, he was content to
remain outside the main stream of poets. He joined the army
in December 1914 and in a diary edited by C. E. M. Joad and
published in 1919 he revealed a complete change that took
place. He turned away from his early idealism. His originality
is the more challenging because so little is known about him.
D. S. R. Welland prints all that can be discovered in his
account in an article in *Renaissance and Modern Essays* (1966) ed.
G. R. Hibbard.

WALT WHITMAN
(1819–1892)
One of the founding fathers of American poetry who is still
read with the highest acclaim. He was born on Long Island
and was already known as a poet before the outbreak of the
Civil War. His volume *Drum Taps* contains many poetic treat-
ments of the war in which he served as a hospital orderly. A
deep compassion and humanity informs all his writing as our
examples show. A considerable literature has been built up
around Whitman. Van Wyck Brooks, *The Times of Melville and
Whitman*, provides a historical perspective.

Further Reading

A great number of books mentioned on pp. 164–79 will be found difficult to obtain. Below appears a short list of general titles that are widely current.

History of the War Decade

G. DANGERFIELD	*The Strange Death of Liberal England* (Paladin)
L. C. B. SEAMAN	*From Vienna to Versailles* (Methuen)
A. J. P. TAYLOR	*English History: 1914–1945* (Oxford)
	The First World War (illustrated) (Penguin)
L. WOLFF	*In Flanders Fields* (Longman)

The Literature of the Decade

B. BERGONZI	*Heroes' Twilight* (Constable)
R. H. ROSS	*The Georgian Revolt* (Faber)
W. K. STEAD	*The New Poetic* (Hutchinson)
P. FUSSELL	*The Great War and Modern Memory* (Oxford)

Some Novels

H. BARBUSSE (French)	*Under Fire* (Dent)
E. HEMINGWAY (U.S.A)	*Farewell to Arms* (Cape)
E. M. REMARQUE (German)	*All Quiet on the Western Front* (Putnam)
H. WILLIAMSON (British)	Various novels under the general title, *A Chronicle of Ancient Sunlight* (Macdonald)

Long Poetic Narrative

DAVID JONES	*In Parenthesis* (Faber)

Discs

What Passing Bell?	(Argo PCP 1074)
Wilfred Owen	(Argo PCP 1075)